MOTHER ROOTS

MOTHER ROOTS

THE FEMALE ANCESTORS OF JESUS

HELEN BRUCH PEARSON

UPPER
ROOM BOOKS®
NASHVILLE

MOTHER ROOTS: THE FEMALE ANCESTORS OF JESUS
© 2002 by Helen Bruch Pearson
All rights reserved.

The Upper Room Web site: www.upperroom.org

Unless otherwise noted, scripture quotations are from the New Revised Standard Version of the Bible. Copyright © 1989 by the Division of Christian Education of the National Council of the Churches of Christ in the United States of America. All rights reserved.

Cover concept: Paige Pearson Beck
Cover art: Carter Bock
Cover design: Bruce Gore
First Printing: 2002

ABOUT THE COVER: The symbolism of roots captures the human rootedness of Jesus. The roots of the female ancestors of Jesus, entwined with other roots, gave birth and sustenance to Jesus. These deep roots, nurtured in unexpected and unpredictable ways, generated new possibilities in life-threatening conditions.

The green found in the tree represents Tamar, the daughter-in-law of Judah. A tall, stately palm tree of ancient Palestine bore the same name and symbolized victory. The red is for Rahab, the prostitute from Jericho. Rahab tied a crimson cord in her window as a sign for Joshua to save her and her family from destruction. Brown symbolizes Ruth who came from the grain-filled plains of Moab and sojourned to Bethlehem, the house of bread. Purple, the royal color, is for Bathsheba, the wife of King David and the first queen mother of Israel.

Library of Congress Cataloging-in-Publication Data

Pearson, Helen Bruch.
    Mother roots: the female ancestors of Jesus / by Helen Bruch Pearson.
        p. cm.
    ISBN: 0-8358-0957-9 (alk. paper)
    1. Jesus Christ—Genealogy. 2. Tamar, daughter-in-law of Judah. 3. Rahab (Biblical figure) 4. Ruth (Biblical figure) 5. Bathsheba (Biblical figure) 6. Women in the Bible. I. Title
    BT314 .P43 2002
    220. 9'2'082—dc21   2002002031

*The narrow-minded ask, "Is this person a stranger
or one of the tribe?" But to those in whom love dwells,
the whole world is but one family.*
—HINDU PROVERB

In recognition of my her-story and family tree,
this book is dedicated

To the loving memory of my roots, my parents
Velma Irene Milem Bruch
(1899–1988)
Page John Bruch
(1898–1980)

In honor of the branches, my siblings
Marjorie Mae Bruch (deceased)
Harriet Fern Bruch (deceased)
Jessie Marie Bruch Weldon
William Bert Bruch
Robert Page Bruch
Ronald Guy Bruch

With thanksgiving for the fruit, my children
Kyle Andrew Pearson
Paige JoAnn Pearson Beck

With hope in the new blossom, my granddaughter
Rachel Marie Pearson

With abiding wonder for the source of constant loving-kindness
in my life, my companion and soul mate,
Luther Edward Smith Jr.

CONTENTS

ACKNOWLEDGMENTS

While the cover of a book may list
only one author, a book is never written
by just one person. Ideas, images, word fragments,
life experiences, empowering presence,
and all the rest that it takes to join sentences
into paragraphs and paragraphs into pages
are always hinged to someone else
and to a larger community.
What I have written in these pages
is connected to persons and communities
beyond myself. Some reside within arm's reach,
offering blessed assurance through their near presence.
Some, scattered throughout the world, have raised
voices of encouragement and goodwill.
They have sought me, and I have been found.
Others have enlisted in the ranks of that great cloud
of witnesses who surround and uphold me.

They continue to teach me long after the end of their earthly lives. They will not let me go, and I am grateful.

Yet it is important to call the names of some who have been my steadfast companions in this writing project, which has taken longer than it seems Methuselah was old. JoAnn Miller, my editor from Upper Room Books, has been both rudder and ballast as she guided, prodded, pushed, and praised this book into being. With humor and tenacity, Rita Collett, project editor extraordinaire, steadfastly guided the book to its publication. Research assistants Shirley Cormicle and Brenda Robertson thoroughly and persistently gleaned periodicals, journals, and books for information about the elusive female ancestors of Jesus. Luther E. Smith Jr., my partner in marriage and all matters of the heart, read and critiqued the manuscript and listened to my explanations and excuses with enduring patience and endearing affection that never ran out. My children, Paige Pearson Beck and Kyle Pearson, along with their spouses, Michael Beck and Christine Baerwalde Pearson, have been generous beyond measure with their love and support. I always receive the faithful affirmation and abiding confidence of my "big sister," Jessie Bruch Weldon, with gratitude. Carol Newsom's critical reading of the manuscript was an invaluable gift to me. Her discerning and erudite comments inspired me to rethink and amend pieces of the text in ways that bring clearer focus to the female ancestors of Jesus and the times in which they lived. I am filled with an overwhelming joy for friends who have kept me close during good times and bad. Among them are Linda Miner, Elaine Eberhart, Sister Patty Caraher, Gilbert (Budd) Friend-Jones, Bob Harris, Juana and Myron McGhee, Kay Keels, Tamar Orvell, Essie Scott, JoAnn Stone, and Barbara Thompson. These and more are cocreators with me. I ask that you remember them when you turn the pages and read the her-stories that lie ahead.

INTRODUCTION

For several years the fact that Jesus' genealogy
according to the Gospel of Matthew lists
four women has intrigued me.
What adds to my interest and wonder
about their introduction as female ancestors
of Jesus is the awareness that
including women in any genealogy
during this period of time was most unusual.
The ancestral mothers of Jesus were
Tamar, Rahab, Ruth, and Bathsheba.
While we know their names,
we know little about these women
and how they felt or what they thought
about the particular situations
in which they found themselves.

USUALLY THE female ancestors of Jesus have been profiled through the men to whom they were connected. They customarily have been researched, interpreted, patronized, and known through the stories about the patriarchs, kings, and warriors by whom they were overshadowed. The overshadowing and overlooking, whether intentional or not, has consistently functioned to diminish or misdirect the truth about these courageous and insistent women who served as vehicles of God's message.

Over the years I have continued to look again and again at the genealogical text and ask my questions: Who were these "outside" antecedents of Jesus? Why did the genealogy include these four women and no more? What plight justified each woman's actions? What was either so virtuous or so sinful about these women that prompted their inclusion in the forty-two generations of the fathers who "begat" Jesus? And why have Christian preachers, pastors, educators, and scholars too frequently overlooked these women's influence on the life and ministry of Jesus?

When asked by Upper Room Books to write a Bible study about Old Testament women as a follow-up to my previous book, *Do What You Have the Power to Do: Studies of Six New Testament Women*, I sensed that here lay the path I had sought. With this challenge came an opportunity to explore the landscapes that had shaped Jesus' ancestral mothers of the Hebrew Bible. In the process of discovering and uncovering their stories, I hoped the female ancestors of Jesus would come forward and disclose themselves to us in all their complexity and be present to us in new and disturbing ways. I expected them to reveal to us their capacity for wisdom that would translate and be relevant for our chaotic times and fragmented lives. I fervently desired that they would re-form our thinking about how they may have inspired and motivated Jesus both to embody and critique his heritage and live out his ministry in radical and unorthodox ways.

Jesus studied the Hebrew teachings as written in the Torah, the five scrolls of Moses. He lived inside the stories of the sacred text with a familiarity that brought close his female ancestors and God's activity in their lives as they related to Israel's sacred history. This book is a Bible study about these female ancestors, the mother roots in Jesus' family tree. Scholarship and research, in partnership with creativity and imagination, open up their stories in transforming and reconciling ways. Freed to become real to us, these women speak to the wider issues of justice and peace in our twenty-first century global society just as they did in ancient Palestine.

While it is a Bible study, this book also is a resource for individual or group spiritual formation and growth as well as an impetus for further engagement with social concerns and issues of human dignity and worth. It is written for persons who prayerfully seek to understand the biblical text beyond the meagerness of the printed words, beyond the limits of gilt-edged pages, and beyond the confining leather cover of the Bible. This book invites readers to listen with integrity for the "more" that remains unspoken between the lines and in the silences of the biblical text, soliciting our patience as we strive to remain faithful and be open to the women who have entrusted their stories to us. The resource asks that we respect the qualities and essential worth that made each woman who she was even as we tell the truth, as far as we can know it, about her external circumstances. This study may sometimes lift us up from the pages of the Bible and place us, not always gently, down inside someone else's perspective. In our brief glimpses of the beckoning possibilities that come to light beyond what we thought we knew, who knows what Mystery yet may find us?

Read with an openness to surprise as you engage in this study. Resist the urge to synthesize; let the biblical text remain discordant and unresolved. As far as possible, do not attempt to make ancient moral and ethical perspectives with all their connotations "fit" contemporary attitudes. Beware of sweeping generalizations and remember that patriarchal culture, society, and religion, which dominated the story lines of the female ancestors of Jesus, were never the same everywhere and in every time. Keep in mind that laws and punishments were not always consistently enforced from age to age and region to region. Be conscious that stories, including those about Jesus' ancestral mothers, tend to be told about extraordinary persons, events, and uncommon behavior rather than about typical, ordinary persons and their everyday lives. Be sensitive to your own perceptual shifts about these women as their stories unfold before you. Take time to look into your heart and the different facets of your personality; probably each of Jesus' female ancestors will already be there waiting for you.

To enter the stories of Tamar, Rahab, Ruth, and Bathsheba on their terms, I have used *midrash* as one way of studying and interpreting the biblical text. Midrash is an ancient means of story-telling and exposition used by Jewish scholars and rabbis to search and re-search the Hebrew Bible. In order to teach the Bible and its lessons orally in ancient times, they told stories based on their best interpretations of the text. The scholars and rabbis asked questions of the text and sought out the meaning behind the words and between the lines to see what was missing—to discover to the best of their ability what had been left out. In their lessons they filled in the blanks, gaps, and silences. With the help of midrash, they made Bible stories relevant to the people.

Using midrash to study and interpret a biblical story is like looking deeply into a multifaceted jewel. As we turn the story again and again, a new facet and another dimension bid our undivided attention. The depth of unending possibilities makes the story a priceless gem. As it is told and retold, searched and re-searched, the story's light from its inner beauty shines forth with revelations that shatter what once seemed so familiar.

So it is with the stories of the female ancestors of Jesus when viewed through the lens of midrash. While the stories themselves remain tethered to the Hebrew Bible and Jewish tradition, the use of midrash provides a means to understand more from the perspective of the ancestral mothers than from the patriarchal fathers. For some, midrash may seem redundant and repetitive, but for the one who expectantly searches the hidden beauty and unexplored facets of the precious gems encapsulated in the stories of Jesus' female ancestors, the turning and re-turning makes good the promise of Jesus: "Ask, and it will be given you; search, and you will find; knock, and the door will be opened for you" (Matt. 7:7).

Midrash without critical scholarship and extensive study makes for good storytelling, but it cannot be counted as authentic biblical interpretation. To retell the stories of Jesus' female ancestors as truthfully as possible, I searched and re-searched the biblical text in several different translations and versions of the Bible. I most often referred to the New Revised Standard Version and the *Tanakh*, the Jewish Bible. Along with the biblical text, I relied upon and critically examined religious journals and periodicals, academic books and materials, Bible commentaries and other interpretive tools. With a balance among critical research, creative midrash, and attentive biblical interpretation, the stories of these women are offered to you.

The scriptures used in Jewish circles, called the Hebrew Bible, are in Christian circles known as the Old Testament. The specifically Christian books of the Bible are called the New Testament. The Christian Bible is divided according to God's original covenant made with the patriarchs of Israel and the new covenant offered by Jesus of Nazareth, the Messiah. The integrity of God's word does not have to be divided arbitrarily between Jewish and Christian theology and thought. Each testament is its own witness to God's salvation history in creation and to God's deeds in the affairs of humankind. With this conviction in mind and with consideration for the faith of the first storytellers, I have used the terms *Hebrew Bible* and *New Testament* throughout the book.

Along with the use of *Hebrew Bible*, I have used two other terms that may need brief explanation. In the stories about the ancestral mothers of Jesus, the Hebrew Bible usually translates any reference to God as LORD, a later translation of Yahweh and perhaps one of the oldest names given to the sovereign God of the Hebrews. Yahweh, or the LORD, was experienced as actively and passionately invested in Israel's particular covenant history. The LORD was the source of Israel's being and the object of love and revelation.

Israel's LORD, like the female ancestors of Jesus, brought about change in unorthodox and unprecedented ways. The LORD, like these strong women, was at the edge and on the boundary, in between times and places, moving people toward a different vision and a new future. The faithfulness of these obedient women reflects the faithfulness of Israel's LORD. From their wombs came forth a new and sometimes abrasive testimony of an inclusive LORD, Yahweh, a God who refused to be confined to human boundaries. We cannot know for certain how these women knew or experienced God or by what name they called God. Their stories were written long after they had returned to dust. However, in keeping with the specific historical and cultural milieus of the women's stories, it seemed appropriate to use LORD as translated when dealing with the texts from the Hebrew Bible.

History has seldom given room for the telling of women's stories in their own right and with their own voices. Most of the biblical texts and stories have come down to us through scribes, editors, and narrators who no doubt were men. In this book when I want to call your attention to the individual and singular story of one of Jesus' ancestral mothers, I generally have used the term *herstory*, my way of lifting her story out of his story. I give tribute and honor to those female ancestors of Jesus who stepped across the pages of his-story into the light of their own her-stories. As these women claim their more unequivocal and radical selves, I rejoice and gladly celebrate their her-stories with them.

The book begins with *The First Word: Introduction*. While this study specifically looks at the mother roots of Jesus as recorded in the Hebrew Bible, it does not overlook the important female ancestor of Jesus named in the New Testament. The book ends with homage and recognition given to Mary, the mother of Jesus, in *The Last Word: Mary's "Yes."* In between *The First Word* and *The Last Word* are six chapters based on the genealogy of Jesus as found in the Gospel of Matthew. Chapter One examines this particular genealogy as one of faith rather than of bloodline and briefly introduces the female ancestors of Jesus named in this genealogy of forty-two generations. Chapter Two presents Tamar, the woman who sought justice. Rahab, a woman who made her faith work for the LORD, is the subject of Chapter Three. Chapter Four examines Ruth, the woman who loved the enemy and expressed God's loving-kindness in an unsolicited manner. Chapter Five tells the story of Bathsheba, a woman who beat the odds, and Chapter Six considers the imprints these matriarchs left on Jesus' family tree and how they may have intersected and influenced the life and ministry of Jesus the Messiah.

Each of the six chapters has seven sections: Locating the Story in the Bible, Ask a Question—Get a Story, The First Turning: Remembering, Her-story Embedded in History, The Second Turning: Reading between the Lines, Women's Rights Are Human Rights, and Ponderings. Introductory words help the reader prepare to study the chapter's material. *Locating the Story in the Bible* briefly discusses the biblical, historical, and cultural context of the woman and the importance of her-story for the developing Israelite nation. *Ask a Question—Get a Story* does just that. In the

Jewish tradition if you ask a rabbi a question, you will get a story for an answer. This section begins with a series of relevant questions about the woman's her-story and then attempts to answer them in a concise and direct reflection.

The First Turning: Remembering employs the process of midrash. In an effort to remember and reassemble the biblical story to reveal more clearly the woman's experience, the story is looked at and told from different angles and directions. To further lift the woman's story from our inherited perspective, *Her-story Embedded in History* seeks to clarify the institutional and historical dynamics in place at the time of the writing of the biblical text. The search for clarity and truth never ends. Because truth, as much as we can discover of it, is always embedded and embodied in events, places, and people in their relationships to one another and God, the complex stories of these women should not be simplified or minimized.

The Second Turning: Reading between the Lines searches the gaps and silences in the text, attempting to see if more truth can be uncovered. I continue to employ midrash as the woman's story receives more thorough scrutiny. Her-story unfolds other facets when turned again and again. In the turning we become aware that many of the cultural situations and social justice issues faced by each woman in her day and time are still with us in the lives of women across our world. *Women's Rights Are Human Rights* excavates these contemporary situations and issues and offers them as challenges to those who would stand side by side with Jesus' female ancestors. *Ponderings* invites the readers to take time to reflect and consider what they have studied in the chapter. As it brings forth the biblical narrative and its multifaceted meanings and implications for living in our day and time, this section serves as a thought provoker for the individual or a discussion starter for a group.

For those who approach this study with a humble heart and in the spirit of truth, an intimate conversation with the ancestral mothers of Jesus awaits. The conversation does not promise to be easy or comforting or to our liking, but failure to engage in the conversation is to miss these righteous and awe-filled women who remind us that God searches out the gaps and spaces where our strongest human resistance has taken hold. Light comes shining into the dark corners and cracks of our preconceived notions about the people God seeks to do God's will. In the gaps and spaces, the corners and cracks, radical seeds of possibility are planted and room is made for the birth of God's own virginal surprises. There a new people is midwifed into being and the hope for a better world grows into God's peaceable realm.

HELEN BRUCH PEARSON
August 18, 2001
Atlanta, Georgia

On this date in 1920, the 19th Amendment to the Constitution was ratified, and women were given the right to vote in the United States of America.

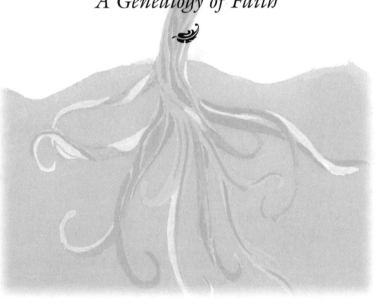

CHAPTER ONE

BACK TO OUR ROOTS

A Genealogy of Faith

Movie
"Simon Birch"
"Rudy"

THE ENTIRETY of the book will focus on the female ancestors of Jesus who are named in the genealogy of Jesus the Messiah according to the Gospel of Matthew (Matt. 1:1-16). Written years after the death of Jesus, the Gospel attributed to Matthew probably was recorded by someone other than the evangelist. Transcribed, translated, and amended through the ages by scribes and scholars, the original manuscript was compiled by a mystery guest. Yet tradition still refers to this New Testament book as the Gospel of Matthew. For easy referencing in this study, any citation made to "Matthew's Gospel," "the Gospel of Matthew," or "Matthew" as the writer follows tradition.

Most Christians know the story of Mary, the mother of Jesus, but do we realize that other women also are named his foremothers? Do we know the stories of Jesus' other ancestral mothers from the Hebrew Bible? *Old Testament* This study will emphasize these four women more than Mary because of our lesser familiarity with them. The names of the female ancestors of Jesus are Tamar (Gen. 38), Rahab (Josh. 2:1-24; 6:17-25), Ruth (the book of Ruth), and Bathsheba (2 Sam. 11–12; 1 Kings 1:11-21, 28-31; 2:13-21; 1 Chron. 3:5).

I invite you now to remember as much as you can about each woman's story in the Bible. Recall all the details you can about the woman, her description, her relationships, and when and where she lived. You may find that you know little about most of these women. Do not be alarmed. This book intends to bring their her-stories forward so that you may get to know them and be empowered by their strong witness about the LORD's faithfulness and loving-kindness.

Locating the Stories in the Bible

Jesus' affirmation and support of women recorded in the Gospel stories radically differ from the prevalent first-century attitudes of Palestine's diverse cultures. As I puzzled about the women Matthew names in his genealogy, I became convinced that he did not mention them coincidentally or accidentally. Genealogies during biblical times usually mentioned women in the lineage only when something out of the ordinary had happened, perhaps something noteworthy about the woman's experience or a perceived irregularity in the lineage among generations. Consequently the names of wives, mothers, and sisters are noticeably absent. The appearance of woman's name probably reflects a social, political, or religious crossroads for a tribe or the entire people of Israel.

In the Bible the recording of a woman's name is a wake-up call to pay attention. Women whose names appear in biblical genealogies were neither weak nor inferior; they demanded recognition from the people with whom they lived. As Christians we seek to be reconciled with them as well, especially with the women named in the genealogy of Jesus the Messiah. Their inclusion signals an important and perhaps irregular event in the history of Israel during their lifetime. Perhaps all these women acted as human points of God's intervention on behalf of Israel and the world. Whatever the point of intervention, its importance connected them to Jesus. These women invite us to discover all we can about who they were and their relationship to the one we call Savior and Redeemer. In our discoveries we may find how much like them we are. They beckon us to stand with them as midwives in the continuing and unfolding birth of Jesus the Messiah in each of our lives.

The lives of Tamar, Rahab, Ruth, and Bathsheba reflect crossroads and turning points in the history of Israel and God's covenant people. These four women take the initiative at absences in the patriarchal lines of descent. They appear when a choice is theirs and make decisions that change the future. God intervenes on their behalf and empowers them to step beyond the patriarchal structure on which they depend. Because the Hebrew religious tradition affirms that God caused each of these women to conceive, generation upon generation believed that its lineage was blessed and sacred. Did these women intuitively know that the male-dominated structure of Israel would someday produce One who would emancipate the whole world?

In a lineage seldom populated by the female gender, these four women help birth "the son of David, the son of Abraham," and "Emmanuel, God-with-us" into the world. Their her-stories testify to God opening and closing wombs and bringing forth patriarchs, kings, and finally the messiah of Israel. Their her-stories confirm that without the intervention of the Israelites' LORD God Almighty, the hoped-for appearance of Jesus the Messiah could not have been accomplished. These women are Jesus' mother roots. Yet their scandalous backgrounds would not inspire most of us to choose them for our ancestors, let alone the ancestors for the Son of God. Why then are they included in the genealogy of Jesus the Messiah?

Ask a Question—Get a Story

Are genealogies in the Bible important and why? Do they serve a theological purpose and if so, what? If Jesus is the Chosen One of

God, why is a human genealogy even necessary? Why does the genealogy in Matthew's Gospel include only four women? (The Gospel separates Mary from the other women in the genealogy.) Why include these four and no more? Who are these four women? How do we explain their presence in a genealogy of fatherly "begats"? If not blood-related to Jesus according to the flesh, what might these women have contributed to his personality and sense of mission? If Matthew considers them important enough to include in the genealogy, why has the Christian tradition given them so little attention in its teachings and traditions? How do we reconcile the gap in Matthew's genealogy between Jesus' blood-line according to the flesh and Mary's conception attributed to the work of the Holy Spirit? Are we given a double genealogy for Jesus—a human and a spiritual genealogy? Since we can prove nothing about Jesus' biological genealogy, does the belief in Jesus as the Messiah ("the son of David, the son of Abraham") really become a matter of faith?

All the New Testament Gospels had their beginnings as oral tradition. Decades after Jesus' crucifixion and resurrection they were written down and collected as literary works. Each addressed a particular audience in an attempt to interpret and explain the theological meaning of particular historical and faith events. No two Gospels are the same. When compared, the four Gospels exhibit many contradictions and inherent differences. The genealogies in the Gospels according to Matthew and Luke offer but one example. Because the religious authorities who collected and assembled the scriptures in what we know as the New Testament decided that no one Gospel was more correct than the others, they included all four as witnesses to both the humanity and divinity of Jesus the Messiah, whom we call Christ.

While Christians believe the Gospels to be timeless embodiments of eternal truths, we must remember that they were not written directly to or for us. Like a river of living water, they flow from one age of believers into another until they come to us. Thus when we read the Gospels, we encounter interpretations that may have come to us through several translations of the original manuscript. While reading the Gospels is inevitably a study about the relativities and fragilities of human history, it is just as inevitably a matter of deep faith that connects our human history with the salvation story of God's abiding presence and loving-kindness in the Hebrew Bible, the New Testament, our present time, and the future yet to come. The mystery of faith is simply this: God has been with us in the past; God promises to be with us in the present; and God has promised to be with us "always, to the end of the age" (Matt. 28:20).

The genealogy in Matthew, as in the Gospel according to Luke, does not stand as a wholly accurate historical or factual document. Genealogical records, rare in the ancient Palestinian world, existed primarily in priestly family records. Otherwise the tangled nature of the genealogies made it impossible to trace ancestral lineage. They were sometimes compressed, skipping entire generations. The absence of common sources for the genealogies of Jesus in Matthew and Luke may explain their inherent internal conflicts. Probably the Gospel writers partially reconstructed their particular records of descent from related genealogies in the Hebrew Bible or other historical documents. They also may have depended on written tradition and oral conjecture.

The fluid Gospel genealogies support the theological perspective and Christological conviction of the writer. Because the writers wrote to and for different audiences, the theological emphases of the Gospels according to Matthew and Luke differ. Not surprisingly then, the genealogies in these two Gospels are inconsistent with each other. Matthew's genealogy purposes to show Jesus as the promised Messiah and ruler of the Jews, connecting Jesus with the Israelite patriarch Abraham and with David, the anointed king of all Israel. On the other hand, Luke maintains a more universal and cosmic lineage for Jesus by connecting him beyond Abraham and Jewish limits and beyond Adam and human limits to conclude that Jesus is none other than the Son of God.

Matthew addressed his Gospel to a people who understood themselves to be a messianic community. Located in a predominantly Jewish milieu, the community comprised of Jews and Gentiles chose to separate themselves from all those who did not believe in Jesus as the Messiah. Jewish roots were affirmed and strengthened as this particular Christian community tried to establish that it was the continuation of God's true covenant people from the time of the patriarchs and matriarchs through the birth of Jesus and even after his resurrection. While the Gospel intended to bracket believers from nonbelievers, equally clear is its message that belief in Jesus the Messiah and not a person's Jewishness becomes the point of inclusion in or exclusion from the community. Given this intent, the genealogy with which Matthew's Gospel begins takes on strategic and theological importance.

The first words of the Gospel according to Matthew alert the reader that what follows is a table of descent or roll of the genealogy of Jesus the Messiah, the son of David, the son of Abraham. Yet it is more than a list of names. It is a narrative about the genesis of Jesus, interspersed with interesting bits of information about some of the ancestors. The story begins with Abraham, through whom God promises to bless all families of the earth (Gen. 12:1-3; 17:5) and moves on through David, the anointed king who will fulfill the Abrahamic promise. But God's chosen king commits sins that infect his kingdom, and over the ensuing centuries Israel falls away in despair and exile.

When it seems that Israel's hope for redemption has been crushed, God reveals a new plan in the birth of Jesus the Messiah. Matthew's Gospel names Jesus as the son of David, which identifies him with royal lineage and places him in the center of Judaism as the messianic "king of the Jews." But Matthew's Gospel also names Jesus the son of Abraham, heir to the promises God made to Abraham: that through him all nations and families of the earth will be blessed and redeemed. Descended in Matthew's Gospel from David and Abraham, Jesus redefines the meaning of kingdom and kingship and enlarges the concept of inclusiveness and chosenness.

The writer of Matthew's genealogy, uninterested in a genetic or biological account or in the accuracy of fact or history, reconstructs Jesus' genealogy to fashion and shape a theological claim and a Christological identity for Jesus within a particular faith community. As Jesus the Messiah, the Christ, the fulfillment of God's purposes and hopes for the world, Jesus of Nazareth is part of a Jewish lineage of promise as well as a spiritual lineage of faith. With this theological and Christological construct, the Messiah is central to God's salvation history, the culmination of all God's promises and purposes for all persons for all time. To underline this promise of inclusivity and to open wide the doors of God's kingdom, Matthew's Gospel deliberately extends Jesus' genealogy to embrace four women.

Tamar, Rahab, Ruth, and Bathsheba were women beset by the implications of scandalous or unconventional sexual unions and questions about their moral integrity. Yet the Gospel of Matthew hints that these women might have foretold the scandalous predicament that surrounded the birth of Jesus the Messiah. The writer of this Gospel is saying that the final outcome of the world in relation to Jesus' birth came through God's initiative, an initiative made manifest in the lives of women whose dubious lives somehow aligned with the divine will.

The First Turning: Remembering

Each of the female ancestors of Jesus entreats us to hear her individual story, to listen through the silences, and to help bring her being and actions into plain view for all to see. The Hebrew Bible portrays the greatest obstacle for women as barrenness, the inability to give birth to sons being the most serious of all tragedies. Consequently stories have come down to us about many Israelite women filled with an inexplicable desire for sons, a desire that rang true for the female ancestors of Jesus as well.

Saying no to motherhood was not an easy option for ancient women, who seem to have been incapable of not desiring sons. After all, the birth of sons brought reward. Within marriage, an institution dominated and controlled primarily by men, bearing sons became the only predictable source of security for women. The women found it advantageous to support a value system that created women in the image the men of Israel desired. Yet stories told about women in the Hebrew Bible may reveal more about the writers' prejudices and fears than about women's lives and their experiences and perceptions of reality.

Motherhood functioned as a major economic factor in Israel's patriarchal culture; both wife and children became assets that would increase a man's property throughout his lifetime. In the Hebrew patrilineal inheritance system only a son could perpetuate and maintain his father's achievements, memory, and family property after the father's death. A son's birth secured continuity of a man's name and property, even as it subordinated the wife and mother.

Although motherhood was an important identity for Jesus' female ancestors, the circumstances leading to the birth of sons often becomes the overarching interest in the narratives. Rather than search out the character of a woman as an empowering and strong role model, the narrative has her disappear from the story soon after the arrival of her son. The story of Rahab offers a limited profile of the ancestral mother whose motherhood is never specifically noted in the Hebrew Bible. Her noteworthiness hinges on Matthew's inclusion of her in Jesus' genealogy.

Under patriarchal influence the biblical narratives rarely presented women as full-fledged human beings in their own right. This study will seek to offer a fuller perspective on the humanity of Tamar, Rahab, Ruth, and Bathsheba, unearthing a more complete understanding of the human roots of Jesus and coming to know and acknowledge his ancestral mothers as the faithful and righteous women they were. Perhaps the greatest challenge lies in finding the "real" women behind the words of the biblical narratives and bringing their her-stories forward as the noteworthy treasures they are.

Her-story Embedded in History

Why does the Gospel narrative include Tamar, Rahab, Ruth, and Bathsheba in the genealogy of Jesus the Messiah, the Christ? Over the centuries scholars have debated this very question without reaching a consensus. The best the world of academia can offer is to report some of the prevailing reasons for the inclusion of these female ancestors of Jesus in Matthew's Gospel and to investigate what, if anything, they have in common.

All four women came from outside Israel's patriarchal family and tribal structure. Tamar and Ruth were foreigners, childless widows. The Israelites, relatives of the Moabite people, reviled the Moabite ancestry of Ruth through Lot and his daughter. Rahab was an alien prostitute. Bathsheba, while married to a Hittite, engaged in adulterous activity (whether forced or not) that resulted in pregnancy and widowhood. The presence of such unusual female outsiders in the genealogy of Jesus may intimate God's intent from the beginning to include Gentiles in the plan of salvation. The inclusion of outsiders in Jesus' lineage may have prepared Matthew's Christian community and church to welcome Gentiles.

The possible and probable sexual activity of all these women has sometimes offended believers, with accusations by many Christian scholars, preachers, and educators about their improper and immoral behavior. However, the Hebrew Bible and later Jewish rabbinic traditions do not regard these women as sinful. They are upheld as women who took redemptive actions on behalf of God's chosen people. Christian commentary frequently has labeled the women in Jesus' genealogy as "exceptional" sinners. Such commentary suggests that Tamar, Rahab, Ruth, and Bathsheba were included in the genealogy to prepare for the advent of Jesus, who came to "save his people from their sins" (Matt. 1:21), and especially to save exceptional sinners like these women. Does this mean that their speciality in sinning separated them from the rest of humanity that Jesus came to redeem? Does this argument suggest that all the men named in the genealogy were without sin?

The male-dominated societies in which Tamar, Rahab, Ruth, and Bathsheba lived have explicitly or implicitly wronged them. Had they not employed initiative, imagination, and sometimes covert or overt manipulation of oppressive and restrictive structures to rectify their situations, they might have forfeited the fullness and freedom of life they finally secured for themselves. Perhaps with their inclusion in the genealogy, Matthew's Gospel gives a slight nod of recognition to women in adverse circumstances, especially those within Israelite patriarchal society.

Notice that the attention of Israelite men makes right the antagonistic and unfavorable situation of each woman: Judah and

David take responsibility for their guilt in relationship to Tamar and Bathsheba. Joshua and Boaz accept responsibility for Rahab and Ruth. In all cases the patriarchal system that has initially wronged them rescues them, giving them and their children an identity, protection, legitimacy, and value. The women and their families eventually support and participate in the patriarchal status quo that has maligned them.

Some scholars concede that Matthew's genealogy may have intended that these women model higher righteousness. Except for Bathsheba, they are foreigners who do not benefit from the few privileges accorded to Israelite women. Yet each of them takes unexpected and surprising action contrary to Israelite customs and traditions to help the covenant people of Israel. Judah, Joshua, Boaz, and David are men in power, but the four female ancestors of Jesus teach all these men a lesson in higher righteousness and cooperation with God.

These four women remind those in power that assumed pre-requisites for God's blessing of salvation do not necessarily exist. While participation in the covenant of the chosen people of Israel supposedly requires purity in one's ancestral line, these women show that blood or birth does not decide participation in God's community of right relationships. A person is invited into relation-ship with God not by physical or biological ancestry but by com-mitting his or her life to God's will and by keeping the faith. The faithfulness and commitment of Tamar, Rahab, Ruth, and Bath-sheba remind us that Christians today are summoned to look for God at work in unanticipated and scandalous ways through those who may be kept outside the congregation of the faithful.

Matthew's genealogy follows the promises of God through the generations from Abraham and David toward the long-expected

Messiah. The inclusion of women may have prepared the hearers and readers for yet another woman and her story of motherhood. Given the her-stories already represented in the genealogy, they might have expected a story about a woman who is wronged. They might not have been particularly shocked by a sexual union that jeopardizes a woman's reputation and leads to a scandal resolved with the birth of a son whom tradition will later legitimate.

While Matthew's audience may have been ready for another woman's story, the hearers probably were not quite prepared for the one that follows. The story of Mary, the final female ancestor of Jesus, is without precedent. Virgin births, already part of the mythic phenomena of some of the ancient Middle Eastern religions, have no basis in the storytelling of the Hebrew Bible. By the time of the Gospel's writing many rabbinic circles considered the female ancestors of Jesus to be distinguished women of virtue because of their assistance to the Jewish people, but not all persons within Judaism or the early Christian church felt this way. Many may have already perceived the Gospel as disgraceful because of the disreputable women Matthew's genealogy included. For them and other leaders within Judaism and the early church, Mary's her-story may have been too scandalous even to consider; God had never before worked this way in the history of the Israelite people.

Prior to Mary's joining the story, God's intervention in the lives of Tamar, Rahab, Ruth, and Bathsheba has been constant but almost hidden. God has actively participated in their her-stories without dismantling structures or shattering traditions. God does not speak or disrupt natural forces. Rather than through the miraculous, God's activity has been realized through human intuition and initiative that fuels a passion for justice and a boldness for righteousness. God blesses the conceptions of these four ancestral women, but each of them conceives in the normal way. Except for these four women, the genealogy traces the lineage of Jesus in the traditional way through the fathers to Joseph. Then everything changes: Joseph, declared to be the husband of Mary, is not the father of Jesus.

With Joseph the paternal lineage, so important in Jewish tradition, stops. The genealogy straightforwardly records that Jesus the Messiah is not born of Joseph but of Mary, leaving Joseph without a son and Jesus without a legitimate father. Jesus, the son of David and the son of Abraham, is not the son of Joseph! Yet according to Jewish tradition, Jesus' adoption into Joseph's line makes him the legal heir to the Davidic kingship: the important theological claim that the writer makes from the beginning. To make such a claim with authority means God has fulfilled the promise through the chain of generations and then has broken the connecting link. The leap over Joseph to Mary sets apart this female ancestor from all others in the genealogy.

Confronted with this wide chasm between the human lineage of Joseph and the overshadowing spiritual conception and birth of Jesus by Mary, the ancient world demanded an explanation for Jesus. No doubt Mary and perhaps Joseph found themselves targets of rumor and malicious slander. The self-proclaimed righteous probably condemned Mary's behavior, and even those who wanted to understand may have suspected her story. Insulting and castigating versions of the story about her conception and Jesus' birth probably made the rounds in the streets and homes and synagogue circles, eventually leading to charges of an illegitimate conception and birth. That Mary has not yet known her husband but some other man is more than scandal; it is behavior deserving of severe punishment.

While the Christian church did not wrestle institutionally with Mary's virginity and the Virgin Birth until a time much later than the composition of the Gospel, certainly insults and diatribes against the Gospel's claims were immediate. (Jewish and Christian writings from the second century C.E. and later, document accusations of Jesus' illegitimacy.) Explanation and acceptance of Mary's her-story as an act of God wait for a later telling in this book. In the meantime remember that for the writer of Matthew's Gospel the position of Jesus the Messiah as David's legal heir is as important as is the manner of his birth. In a Gospel written for use by and in the church, the writer demonstrates the belief that in the birth of Jesus, "Emmanuel, God-with-us" is born and will continue to be with the church "always, to the end of the age" (Matt. 1:23; 28:20).

The Second Turning: Reading between the Lines

In this study of the female ancestors of Jesus, I employ a way of interpreting and writing about scriptural texts and stories called *midrash*. A responsible and disciplined effort to understand and explain the Bible in order better to comprehend with head and heart the ancient texts, midrash has helped me find answers to old questions. Years ago I started wondering about some of the biblical texts, about why the women were generally silent and without voice. I wondered who got left out and why. Most of all I wondered if I might dare to use my God-given imagination to fill in the unexplained gaps in many of the stories.

I began asking questions of the texts. If I read between the lines, what unrevealed aspects of God might surprise me? Behind the written words, hidden from easy view and waiting in the shadows, what sort of God might I find? I discovered that these kinds of wonderings made some people nervous and uneasy; my questions were not always welcomed. Yet I believed that if Christians professed faith in a God who continues to reveal and make things fresh and new, it becomes our responsibility to keep asking about this God who is more than we can ever comprehend. We must keep searching for this God who can never be completely known within the words of sacred texts.

While still wondering and asking questions, I discovered that Judaism's ancient tradition of honoring the imagination as a gift from God found expression in the process of midrash. Midrash, an ancient yet contemporary Jewish method of study, examines and interprets the sacred texts in light of current circumstances. Midrash intends to seek, inquire, and demand meaning from the scripture. Always starting with the biblical text, midrash then asks questions in an effort to fill in gaps and to make sense of what is omitted or unanswered by the text, searching and re-searching the text and pushing its meaning as far as the imagination can conceive. Midrash turns the biblical text upside down, inside out, and outside in. People look at the words and stories in diverse ways, turning them until they become alive and real. Midrash is a way to come to God, know God intimately, be close to God, and feel God's presence. For Judaism midrash begins where the biblical text ends, and it is based on the understanding that any law or story or commandment in scripture immediately raises questions that call for comment and further interpretation and that result in more possible insights. As the rabbis and sages plumbed the depths of the sacred texts, the more inexhaustible and extravagant they realized were the imagination and mystery of God. These midrashic insights and interpretations were accumulated in written collections of the discourses of the sages and rabbis across the ages. In them we encounter an early rabbi's teaching about the divine word: "Turn it, and turn it again. Never stop turning it, for everything is contained in it."

Midrash spins and weaves new stories and ideas out of the threads of the original story—always with the possibility that a more complete tapestry will emerge. It never claims that the subject of interpretation and reinterpretation actually happened or is literally true. But when the stories are peeled back layer by layer, and the imagination is used to get at what may have been left unsaid and what may be implied behind the written words, more truth may yet come forth. Just because the text does not record it does not mean that our discoveries between the lines are not true.

The use of this largely unfamiliar form of interpretation as a responsible way of expounding and expanding the meaning of scripture is a challenge to Christians. To re-search God's word, to demand new meaning for our day and time, is to risk liberating the scriptures from our sometimes dull and predictable interpretive mind-set. Midrash requires our openness to hear the biblical texts as if for the first time and to see them in fresh and new contexts. The process asks us to use critical scholarship balanced with imagination and creativity to tell again the old stories in order to get to more of their meanings. Because the Holy Spirit never runs dry in our efforts to understand, this kind of retelling keeps the scriptures from becoming stagnant and the radicality of God ever before us.

Because midrash does not require theological training or expertise in the discipline of higher biblical criticism, readers need not depend totally on resources outside themselves in studying the scriptures. Midrash allows them to approach the biblical text as holy ground without the constraints of an approved academic process. To all who earnestly desire to know God, midrash is a resource that opens the possibility for better understanding and interpreting textual meanings. It provides an opportunity for those who thirst after the living Word to drink deeply as they fill in gaps and make smooth the rough places and mine the sparse words of the text. Midrash gives ordinary Christians the responsibility to trust themselves as they search for the multilayered meanings implanted in biblical stories. We are asked to consider midrash as seriously as we do the Greco-Roman philosophy upon which so much of the Christian church in the West has built its theology and doctrines and upon which it has come to depend for interpreting sacred texts.

In using the process of midrash as a way of getting at the her-stories of Jesus' female ancestors, I felt free to ask questions of the text. And in the asking, I found a way through the silences to discern some answers to my questions. In this study, I have balanced my interpretation through midrash with critical research that sought out and used various and plausible sources of biblical scholarship. I have done so hoping to break open and free the voices of these women we call the ancestral mothers of Jesus.

I invite you to join me in using midrash as a lens through which to view more of the her-stories of Tamar, Rahab, Ruth, and Bathsheba. Looking at the stories from many different angles, we will examine what we have received in the scriptures. We will search and re-search the stories, making the same demands of them as did Jacob when he wrestled with the angel. We will not let them go until they bless us. Using midrash as one form of interpretation, let us be responsible and diligent in our efforts to understand more about the text as we probe its depth. However, let us also read between the lines and bridge the gaps and silences as we ask questions and seek answers to what remains hidden about the lives of these women. As we use our God-given imaginations to spin and weave new meanings out of the old tapestry, we will approach these her-stories as sacred text and with persistence and insistence keep turning and turning the text. What appears to be the simple truth is rarely all the truth, and it is never simple.

As we use our minds to engage in both rigorous scholarship and inventive midrash, I hope we may discover insightful and inciteful things about these women and about ourselves. While all we find may not be written in the text, it may nonetheless offer more truth about who these women really were. God has told us over and over again, "I am about to do a new thing; now it springs forth, do you not perceive it?" (Isa. 43:19). Midrash commits us to look for the new that is promised in the old. It awaits us in the reinterpretation of these her-stories about the mother roots of Jesus. Let us pray that our spirits will be enlarged as we open ourselves to the work of the Spirit that makes all things holy.

Women's Rights Are Human Rights

The Bible does not reflect a monolithic history and institutionalization of Judaism or Christianity or a one-dimensional view of women. These sacred writings reflect various evolutions of historical, cultural, political, and religious values and beliefs over different periods of time. The priestly view of women dominant in the biblical texts and in the Hebrew laws may not have been the most widely held or characteristic view of women in the larger Israelite culture. Recorders of the biblical texts wrote from different life settings and orientations, and contrasting values and attitudes emerge even among Israelite communities during a single period of time. The divergent life settings and attitudes toward women and the possible options that might have been available to some women in their individual contexts are occasionally found in the biblical texts. Still, if alternative views of women and their roles, positions of leadership, and modes of religious expression and rituals existed, they generally have been seamlessly edited out and excluded from the canon of scripture.

As students of the biblical text, we must always think about what may have been edited out and excluded about women though remaining cautious about making generalizations and drawing unsupported conclusions or superimposing our contemporary assumptions and values upon the ancient cultures from which these women came. Biblical narration is seldom, if ever, told from the woman's perspective. Testimony about the actual experiences of women—what they knew, what they thought, how they felt, and what they valued and loved—has come to us through the literary work of scribes and priests rather than through the voices of women themselves. While we exercise integrity in our investigation of the her-stories of women, we are charged also to remember that what was written and included in the biblical narratives never completely covered what really happened or what life was actually like for the ancestral mothers of Jesus.

We may lament the dearth of information we have about the life and times of biblical women, but there still is enough for us to glimpse their extraordinary and phenomenal lives. Because of what we do know, we wonder not so much about whether Tamar, Rahab, Ruth, and Bathsheba enacted God's will as how their stories were told and interpreted down through the ages of Judaism and Christianity. And what of today?

The female ancestors of Jesus may be dangerous women who reveal the complexities of our human hearts and minds and shadow sides, which we go to great lengths to hide. They may call into question our commitment to the work of justice as they affirm that goodness, righteousness, and faithfulness are more than acts of simple obedience to inherited, secondhand morality that too often fails to bring transformation and generativity to the people of God. Their presence may remind us that women like themselves still live among us today. Tamar, Rahab, Ruth, and Bathsheba can be found in rural villages across the face of the earth. They make their homes in towns and cities, eke out a living in ghettos and slums, suffer domestic violence and abuse in our neighborhoods. They live in the darkest alleys and on the crowded streets and populate refugee camps and prisons. Sometimes they sit beside us in our places of prayer and worship.

Tamar of today still searches for fragile justice that depends on the decisions of men to keep or break laws supposedly designed for her protection. She still risks punishment and unfair treatment in a judicial system supposedly designed to guarantee her equal rights and freedom under the law. Rahab the prostitute of today still lives and works the streets wherever men will pay for what she offers. Misunderstood by many, she still looks for a way to save her family and all that belongs to her, still desires to dwell among a people who will offer her a better way. Ruth of today continues to journey as an alien, seeking refuge in a foreign country among a people she does not know, a religion she does not understand, and a language she does not speak. Too often her only way to obtain food and shelter is to glean from a welfare system that perpetuates her marginalization. Bathsheba of today continues to be victimized by authorities who take advantage of her beauty. She remains battered, abused, and wrongly accused.

These women live among us today, and they will not remain silent and invisible forever. Some day they will refuse to be seamlessly edited out and generally excluded because of who they are. If not today, then perhaps tomorrow they will threaten and make uneasy the hierarchal and patriarchal institutions of the world as they choose life for themselves and their children. They will stand at the crossroads and challenge the church's complacency in fulfilling its prophetic mission. Perhaps God will intervene on behalf of a hurting and hungering creation and once again empower the scandalous Tamars, Rahabs, Ruths, and Bathshebas of today to midwife a new spirit among us. Perhaps then in the cave of our hearts and the silent night of our lives we will be prepared to receive again the birth of Jesus the Messiah, the Christ, the anointed One.

Ponderings

Please take time to reflect on and ponder what you have read and studied in this chapter. The following questions and comments are intended to assist you. They may serve as discussion starters for group study, or they may be sources for contemplation and examination for individual use. Perhaps they will prompt further study and/or action. Through them you hopefully will bring forward the multifaceted meanings and implications of this chapter for living in our day and time.

1. Perhaps the readers and hearers of the Gospel genealogy of Jesus found it more believable with a few women included rather than all women excluded.

    •   After you read *The First Turning: Remembering*, what surprised you about Tamar, Rahab, Ruth, and Bathsheba's inclusion in Jesus' genealogy? *that they do appear*

    •   Which of these women would you choose to include and honor in your lineage, and why? *Ruth   She is admirable in so many ways!*

    •   If they were your ancestral mothers, which of their stories would you pass on to your children?

    Your responses to these questions may help you understand why the presence of these women in Jesus' lineage has troubled readers throughout the centuries.

2. Judaism considers it the responsibility of a good Jew to read and ask questions of the sacred texts as long as the text itself is not negated. Judaism gives believers permission to use their imaginations to fill in the blanks and to interpret what might be hidden between the lines.

    •   How has your religious education encouraged you to ask questions of the Bible and to use your imagination as an interpretive tool? to ponder other viewpoints? *I guess it really has not.*

- As your understanding of the Bible has broadened and deepened, what has helped you understand your responsibility to listen in the intervals of silence found in the text?

  see what God wants me to glean from the text

3. The intent of midrash is to seek, inquire, and demand meaning from the scriptures.

   - What do you think about the use of midrash as a method of studying and interpreting the Bible? *interesting new to me*

   - In what ways does its searching, re-searching, and pushing the meaning of the text make you uneasy? *accuracy*

   - How does using your creativity and imagination as a resource for study and interpretation challenge your current approach? *takes me out of a relative comfort zone.*

4. In her book *The Red Tent*, author Anita Diamant uses midrash to explore the story of Dinah in the book of Genesis. Dinah was the daughter of Jacob and a sister of Judah (the father-in-law of Tamar and the father of Tamar's two sons). Diamant makes Dinah the narrator of the story after her rape, and Dinah's voice provides a picture of the daily life, domestic routines, and religious traditions of Jacob's nomadic tribe. In the book menstruating women are confined at a place called the "red tent."

   Probably something like a "red tent" was the place of segregation and confinement for women during Israel's early tribal history. Perhaps this time apart became a welcomed sanctuary for women. Here, away from the domination and authority of the men of the tribe, they confided in one another and spoke their hearts' secrets and concerns. They passed on information and advice, affirmed one another, and found companionship that refreshed and restored. They experienced freedom from all the expectations and demands of a patriarchal culture. In the "red tent" women connected with one another in profound relationships of nurture and care. Western cultures have few places like the "red tent" where women make life-giving and restorative connections with other women.

- Where is your "red tent?" *sisters in Christ from church, by blood, + internet friends*
- Whether you are male or female, in what ways does a "red tent"—a sanctuary for retreat and speaking your heart's secrets and concerns—appeal to you? *at some times usually*
- Where might you cultivate sustaining and caring relationships? *retreat, Bible study*

5. Government, religious organizations, and faiths still debate women's rights that move the female population toward full equality.

    - In what ways does your culture segregate and confine women to their places? *some churches*

    - *Business world* In what arenas are women not given equal access or treatment? Consider the hiring and promotion practices of some corporations and private industries, the issue of equal pay for equal work.

    - How does your faith tradition segregate, confine, or exclude the participation of women? How does it welcome and fully celebrate the diversity of gifts within its female membership?

6. Although often viewed as scandalous within the biblical text, the names of Tamar, Rahab, Ruth, and Bathsheba are written boldly and without apology in Jesus' genealogy. They are the spiritual mother roots of the Christian Messiah. Our ability to understand who they were and why they were included in the genealogy of Jesus challenges us to come to terms with who we are. These female ancestors of Jesus were women who made themselves available to God just as they were. They were real.

They teach us that we do not have to leave behind who we are in order to receive God's acceptance. Even that which we choose to reject or condemn about ourselves these women affirm God compassionately dignifies and blesses. Their her-stories confirm that God desires all of who we are—even the parts of ourselves that we want to keep secret or hidden. These ancestral mothers of Jesus testify that social and moral exile cannot hold hostage God's blessings of love, justice, and peace. They bear witness that individuals who are oppressed and disempowered by social and religious structures, when touched by God, become instruments of healing, hope, and reconciliation. They remind us that redemption and transformation do not depend on our perfection but on our response to God's love and desire for us.

In our world today, men and women seek in desperate and scandalous ways to find their voices and places. In spite of oppression and disempowerment, they struggle to obtain what is rightfully theirs—freedom, shelter, food, safety, justice, and companionship.

- As Christians, how might we support, assist, and affirm those who would take their places alongside the unsung female ancestors of Jesus?

- Do you think it is ever a mandate for Christians to break moral, social, or legal codes in order to secure human rights and human dignity for those who cannot remove themselves from the grip of tyranny, torture, violence, and submission? Why?

- What are your guidelines for such actions?

- What advice might Jesus' female ancestors offer you from their experiences?

- What is your response?

CHAPTER TWO

TAMAR

A Woman Who Sought Justice

Before reading the chapter, take time to remember as much as you can about Tamar's story in the Bible: who she was, her description, her relationships, and when and where she lived. Then read Genesis 38; Ruth 4:11-12; and Matthew 1:3*a*.

Locating the Story in the Bible

We find Tamar's story in the book of Genesis, also known as the book of "origins" or "beginnings." Genesis divides naturally into two main parts. The primeval history (chapters 1–11) tells about the world's origin and the creation of humankind. The time of the patriarchs, the ancestral history, and the Israelites' journey into Egypt make up the rest of Genesis (chapters 12–50). These last chapters recall the remarkable experience of the mysterious adoption by the sovereign and mighty LORD of Israel's ancestors, selected to found a holy nation and to bring into existence a chosen people. Genesis transitions the reader of the biblical text from primeval to patriarchal history with intrigue after intrigue.

The fact that the first book of the Bible retains Tamar's story indicates her importance in relationship to the rest of the narratives in the Hebrew Bible. Probably a man of high position and authority recorded it as part of the biblical text. It is ironic that such a man would include the story of a woman with no authority who outwits and tricks a man of great authority, the patriarch and leader of the Twelve Tribes. The Bible generally presents the patriarchs as righteous and holy, and since Judah is not always cast in a positive light in relation to Tamar, it is even more surprising that the story remained in the Bible.

The chapter that brings Tamar into our view is part of the ancestral history. Even if the story is not chronological history, it still sheds light on the Hebrews' perception of their LORD's work in human history. The story of Tamar offers glimpses of moral and ethical values in a particular religious culture during a particular time of its development, reflecting specifically the primary place of the patriarch and some roles of women within the tribe. Although it cannot be dated with absolute accuracy, the story of Tamar, first orally told and retold over the centuries, probably originated sometime between 1500 and 1200 B.C.E. Tamar's her-story occurs in the text after Joseph is sold into slavery and concludes before Jacob and his sons sojourn into Egypt because of a terrible famine and before they are reunited with Joseph. Its strategic placement makes it a fascinating insertion into the complete Joseph story.

Tamar's story cannot be separated from the larger story of the Hebrews or from the individual stories of the patriarchs recorded in Genesis, among them Jacob and his son Judah. The Bible mentions Tamar two other times. On Boaz's announcement that he intends to marry Ruth from Moab, the people and the elders of the town pronounce this blessing: "May your house be like the house of Perez, whom Tamar bore to Judah" (Ruth 4:12). The Gospel according to Matthew notes that Judah is the father of Perez and Zerah by Tamar (Matt. 1:3a). Tamar, according to this Gospel, is an ancestral mother of Jesus the Messiah.

Ask a Question—Get a Story

What do we know about Tamar? Who was she behind the veil that covered her face? Did she wear any other masks to survive? Will we ever get to know what she longed for or what she feared? From where did her "chutzpah" (boldness) come? Was she a trickster who deceived the one who intended to deceive her? Why did she tire of being a victim? Was she righteous or morally corrupt? What are we to remember about Tamar?

The text tells us that Tamar was a righteous daughter-in-law, wife, and widow. As a woman wronged, Tamar determined to bring about justice for herself and Judah's tribe. A woman of courage, Tamar pushed the boundaries of tribal law. In this ancient Hebrew culture, women took their identity from the men who controlled their lives and treated them like property, but Tamar took on her own identity—and what an identity it was! Tamar was the name of a magnificent and imposing palm tree in the ancient Near East. It signified victory. Perhaps the woman Tamar was tall and graceful like the date palm. As her story unfolds, she becomes for us a sign of victory even when the odds turn against her. *Is she a sign of victory?*

The Hebrew Bible tells us that Judah, the son of Jacob and patriarch of his own tribe, got Tamar as a wife for his firstborn son, Er. That Judah "got" Tamar to be his son's wife probably means he offered a bridal price for Tamar or reached some other agreement with her father. With few rights of their own during this period in Hebrew history, women remained under the authority first of their fathers and then their husbands—handed down, handed over, and sometimes handed back. This structure of authority becomes part of Tamar's experience as a woman in the tribe of Judah.

Beyond the information found in the biblical text, we are challenged to imagine faithfully what might have happened to Tamar and to hear the part of her-story that was never told. We are called to move into the loose space of wonder and sit quietly in the silence, to wait between the inhaling and exhaling of our breath for Tamar to approach us. Perhaps in the space between Tamar's long ago "then" and our present "now," she will make herself known to us. Perhaps Tamar will meet us between the lines and in the gaps of the story, and we will engage in dialogue. Perhaps we will see and hear as if for the first time, and together with Tamar we will break open the Word of life and have a feast.

The First Turning: Remembering

Judah had just instigated selling his youngest brother, Joseph, to Ishmaelite traders and had deceived his father into believing that his favorite son was dead. Soon after, Judah left his father and brothers and camped in an area of Adullam. Although Hebrew law and traditions clearly preferred marriage to a woman within the Hebrew community, Judah needed sons to help with the labor required to work the land. He needed a wife, so he married the daughter of a Canaanite man. We never learn her name; we know her only as daughter, wife, and mother. She and Judah had three sons. Judah named the firstborn Er, and his wife named the other two Onan and Shelah.

When it came time to find a wife for Er, the firstborn, Judah got Tamar, a non-Hebrew—probably a Canaanite raised in a polytheistic culture where goddess worship was common. Required to give up her identity as her father's daughter, Tamar joined a tribe with laws and customs strange to her. She was the foreigner. She came into a closed family circle that believed in a different deity from the local gods and goddesses of her heritage. Her new family had rules about cleanliness and marriage that differed from those of her culture. Although Judah, as patriarch, assumed responsibility for Tamar as a member of the tribe, she aggressively had to make a place for herself. The surest way to security was to give birth to many male children. Until Tamar produced a son, she was cut off from the only position of honor and status available to her. Being an outsider and still barren made her suspect, not a "real" member of the tribe.

Although Er's name meant "protector," he was a bad man—so bad that we can only imagine the circumstances of Tamar's life with him. While we do not know how Er exposed or endangered himself before the LORD, we do know that his wickedness displeased the LORD, who ended Er's life before Tamar could conceive. To be childless and a widow in any situation was tragic but particularly so for Tamar, who was already marginalized in the tribe. With the death of Er, one destined to become the patriarch of the tribe, childless Tamar became an object of pity. Judah had supposed that this "date palm" would bear the sweetest fruit for his son and the tribe of Judah. Instead his firstborn son lay dead.

Hebrew law gave Tamar, now a levirate widow, some rights and security that she otherwise would not have had. In keeping with the levirate law, Judah sent his second-born son to join with Tamar (Deut. 25:5-6). This law decreed that the next living brother, Onan, would provide offspring for his dead brother. The levirate duty of the next brother and the widow was to bear a son to ensure the continuation of the dead husband's name and lineage. The levirate law demanded that Tamar have sexual relations with her brother-in-law until the birth of her first son. This was considered an act of devotion for the dead husband.

The Hebrews during the time of Tamar did not believe in life after death or any kind of resurrection. The souls of the dead were confined throughout eternity to Sheol, the abode for all the dead. For these ancient people male children offered the only hope of continued existence after death, guaranteeing that the family name would be preserved among the living and that a father would be honored and his memory kept alive. More sons on earth meant more status in Sheol. Judah clearly had an investment in seeing that Onan fulfilled the levirate bond.

Judah sent Onan to Tamar and referred to her only as "your brother's wife." Never did Judah call Tamar by name. There was no need. When Tamar married into the tribe, she gave her allegiance to Judah. Onan, neither stupid nor wise, lacked compassion and was cold and calculating. He knew the birth of a son to Tamar would diminish his share of inheritance: the more descendants the less inheritance. Forget the levirate law—this was an economical matter for Onan. The idea of sharing the family's inheritance with his dead brother's child, whom he had fathered, was not at all attractive to Onan. But the prospect of having sex with Tamar was apparently quite appealing. *where is there any indication of this*

Each time Onan had intercourse with Tamar, "he spilled his semen on the ground" and let it go to waste. While a primitive form of birth control, it worked. Each week and month that passed without Tamar's having conceived diminished her status in the tribe. She knew she would never get pregnant this way, but she had little recourse. If Tamar reported Onan's actions to Judah, Onan would not likely admit to it. She was not in the wrong, but she was trapped. Onan did not tell Judah he had no intention of keeping the levirate law. Though Onan appeared to be fulfilling his duty with Tamar, she remained barren; the assumption could only be that she was at fault. Had anyone known about Onan's deception the judgment against him would have been severe, for to waste his seed would have been perceived as a threat to the tribe and considered an act almost as serious as murder. Onan, aware of the seriousness of his deception, persisted. His response to Tamar was cruel and his disobedience to the levirate law blatant.

In her already tenuous position in the tribe, Tamar must have felt that she was all alone. The biblical text tells us this was not the case. The LORD sided with the woman—a Canaanite woman at that. Displeased, in fact, angry, about Onan's greed over inheritance and his refusal to obey the levirate law, the LORD took Onan's life also. Divine justice came quickly for Onan, but the LORD did not strike down Tamar.

What was Judah to think? Two of his sons had died after sexual intimacy with Tamar. His hopes to keep his tribal name alive through them after his own death were dead, and his youngest son Shelah was not old enough to fulfill the levirate obligation. Judah wondered if he should blame Er and Onan for their surprise endings—but for what? Or was Tamar the cause of their deaths? Often in ancient patriarchal Israel what a man did not understand or did not want to claim responsibility for was assigned to evil spirits and ungodly forces.

wonderings
probably not
directed at
his sons

The Hebrew cultic structure sometimes reinforced the perception of women's negative powers. Judah suspected that Tamar possessed potent and mysterious powers that had killed his sons. She was a Canaanite; and although she had been in his Hebrew tribe for some time, perhaps she was not yet fully converted to the Yahwist ways. Perhaps she still practiced some pagan ways of her kin. Unable to see any fault with his sons and uncertain about whom to blame, Judah chose to blame the childless widow. For him Tamar was an awkward inconvenience and a burden. Judah probably never intended to give her to his son Shelah as commanded in the levirate law, so he sent her back to her father's house with these words: "Remain a widow in your father's house until my son Shelah grows up." Perhaps Judah saw this as a final solution for himself, but he presented it as a tentative measure to Tamar.

supposition, of course

"Remain a widow"—a death sentence for Tamar. To be sent away from the tribe and returned to her father's house seemed an

untenable and precarious situation for Tamar. She had long heard
from the tribal elders: "The law decrees...." She knew the levirate
law decreed that Judah was to give her to Shelah or release her
from the levirate bond, one or the other. But Judah did neither. As
long as Judah had a son, he had no right to turn her away and give
her back to her father, an act of total rejection on Judah's part and
an even greater humiliation for Tamar.

No longer a virgin, Tamar returned to her father's household
not as wife or mother but as a childless widow. Bound by the levirate law and betrothed to Shelah without the freedom to marry,
Tamar was confined to her father's house and under his control
again. Imprisoned as a betrothed childless widow, Tamar was an
outcast not only in her father's household but within Judah's tribal
structure as well. When men made the rules, women frequently
suffered the consequences.

Long after Judah sent Tamar to stay as a widow in her father's
house, Judah's wife died. Tamar knew that Shelah, to whom she
had been promised, had grown up, but Judah had not returned
her to the tribe. She heard that Judah was planning an outing with
his good friend Hirah the Adullamite. After Judah's required
mourning period, the two men went up to the sheepshearing fes-
tival not far from the house of Tamar's father. Judah had to pass
by the entrance to Enaim on his way to Timnah to reach the sheep-
shearers. Enaim was at the crossroads in an open place, and one
could see travelers approaching from a distance.

Tamar had not forgotten Judah's promise to fulfill the levirate
law, nor had she forgiven him for his treatment of her. For Tamar,
the need to bear a son who would perpetuate her dead husband's
name and inheritance and provide her with security overrode all
other life concerns. In honoring that past relationship, Tamar
believed she would fulfill her highest moral obligation and tribal
responsibility. Perhaps tired of having men make decisions for

her—tired of being given away and then given back, tired of being told what to do and where to go—Tamar finally refused to be the victim. Judah might have patriarchal authority, but she was not powerless. She would not be intimidated or ignored. She would not be shut out or shut up. She would not allow Judah's unfair and humiliating treatment of her to ruin her life. *was her scheme also not ruining her life*

While Tamar could not change her father-in-law's attitude or his tribal authority, she could attempt to change her situation. She became her own agent for justice and made the levirate law work for her. Marginalized by culture and religion, Tamar used wit, logic, and courage to obtain what was rightfully hers in the first *hmmm* place. Firmly resolved to force Judah to take responsibility for her, Tamar took off her widow's clothes and draped a veil over her face and body and wrapped herself up. Veils were more than a face covering for Hebrew and Canaanite women. Often they were stole-like ornamental coverings that were draped around the body as well. Hebrew women wore a veil as the mark of a marriageable virgin and removed it in connection with the marriage ceremony.

The kind of veil Tamar used and the reason she chose to wear it are not clear. While she was not a marriageable Hebrew virgin or a consecrated woman of the temple, with Tamar's face veiled, would Judah know that? After the drab harshness of widow's garb, perhaps it felt good to be draped in a veil of soft, flowing gossamer material. Veiled, draped, and feeling alive, Tamar left her identity in a heap among the widow's clothes. From this point on her every movement went beyond the acceptable boundaries for a Hebrew widow. Transformed and decisive, she started for the crossroads.

Although we do not know all the details of Tamar's intentions or of her appearance, she certainly planned to confront Judah. Without any guarantees she moved ahead courageously and boldly, hoping the confrontation would right the wrong that had been done to her.

Though the biblical text never indicates that Tamar presented herself as a prostitute (temple or otherwise) who sought to allure, solicit, or seduce Judah, commentators have assumed that because Judah thought she was a prostitute, she must have been dressed as one. But Judah saw what he wanted to see and what suited his needs at the time. Widowed for about a year and on vacation from his tribe, he could trust his good friend Hirah not to divulge his behavior. Although Hebrew law ruled against taking a prostitute, Judah discovered here by the side of the road what seemed an available, desirable woman. With no attempt at flattery, Judah did not ask; he demanded. He was a man of power and authority; this was business.

Judah failed to recognize his daughter-in-law, and Tamar let Judah believe what his expectations and desires led him to imagine. Tamar probably was not surprised at Judah's demand. Having known two of his sons and having lived in the tribe for several years, she undoubtedly knew Judah's habits. But had she really prepared herself for this? Perhaps this was going too far. Perhaps she should reveal her identity to Judah. She had hoped to meet Judah, but in this way? Yet she knew the truth and her rights as prescribed by the levirate law, and she did not believe that Judah planned to uphold the law. Perhaps this encounter promoted justice and righted the wrong of Judah's deception. Perhaps, the LORD willing, in this turn of events Judah himself would give her a son and make good the levirate law.

If Judah wanted a prostitute, Tamar would give him a prostitute. But before committing to his demand, Tamar asked Judah what he would pay to have intercourse with her. He proposed to send her a kid from his flock, a substantial proposition—a generous offer any prostitute would consider. The seal Judah wore on a cord around his neck and the staff he carried indicated that he was no common Canaanite but a Hebrew patriarch. He could afford the price. Besides, Judah was proud that he was not cheap. He wanted this woman to know her good fortune in his having chanced upon her.

Having been deceived once by Judah, Tamar was not ready to be deceived again. She agreed on the price but negotiated that Judah leave a pledge with her until the delivery of the kid: Judah's seal, cord, and staff. Judah hesitated. Leaving them with Tamar would mean he would be without the symbols of his authority. But everyone in the region knew who he was. While he used the seal to imprint his signature on important documents and clay tablets, he knew the woman could not use it. The seal, with its patterned cord, signified his identity—not hers. He could have others made. He depended on his staff for support and occasionally for defense; he might miss it during the next few days but the enticing prospect made for an easy decision. If worse came to worst, he could borrow a staff from Hirah.

There was really nothing sacred about what happened next. With the business deal successfully transacted by the roadside, Judah had sexual intercourse with Tamar. Just like that, and it was over. But Judah left more with Tamar than just the pledge, and Tamar took more from Judah than just his seal, cord, and staff. Unknown to either of them, she had conceived. That one brief sexual encounter with Judah changed Tamar's life forever.

Ancient Hebrew culture believed that any pregnancy involved the LORD's action. The culture understood that the physical act of intercourse had something to do with getting pregnant, but all the biological conditions for conception were not yet known. Conception was still a mystery that required the LORD's blessing. Ever since marrying into the tribe, Tamar had heard about the LORD's promise to Father Abraham that the chosen people would become a mighty nation from whom kings would come (Gen. 17:6). Tamar knew that Judah had no sons beyond Shelah to carry on his bloodline, which threatened Judah's legacy. Through the levirate law she knew she should bear a son to perpetuate Judah's lineage and her dead husband's name. Tamar did not have intercourse with Judah for personal pleasure or profit or because she was ordered to. With sacred intent Tamar acted to preserve the name and inheritance of her dead husbands, Judah's sons. Trusting her life to the LORD of the Hebrews, Tamar believed that justice and redemption would come to her. *revenge ∠ OR*

Just when Judah thought all was well, he received disturbing news: his daughter-in-law had behaved like a common whore and was with child as a result of her misconduct. Judah apparently did not want Tamar betrothed to his only remaining son. He had blamed her for the death of his two sons and sent her back to her father's house. Judah, her father-in-law, had shirked his responsibility by withholding the unsandaling ceremony that would have released her from the levirate bond and given her freedom to marry outside the tribe (Deut. 25:7-10). Tamar's pregnancy had brought dishonor to his name and disgrace to the tribe, and Judah was angry.

The writer has given us hints all along about the tenuous and fragile state of Judah's tribe. Tamar was the only present possibility for ensuring the tribe's survival. We also know who impregnated her by the roadside, but Judah did not have this information. Judah only knew that the child Tamar carried was not fathered by either of his dead sons. Even if he remembered Tamar's essential role in the continuance of his lineage, Judah would willingly sacrifice Tamar to save face and retain his position of authority.

Without hesitation Judah said, "Bring her out, and let her be burned"—an extraordinary death sentence even for that time (Lev.

20:14; 21:9). Although death by stoning was the usual punishment for adultery, Judah, as the unquestioned patriarch of the tribe, could pronounce whatever punishment he felt suited the crime. Judah may have abused her and used her in life, but Tamar was not ready to be put to death. She had chosen life, and she intended that she and her descendants would live (Deut. 30:19). Having firsthand knowledge about power, Tamar, in that critical moment, moved from simply knowing about the use of power to using assertively the power of her knowing. She knew what she was going to do. She would have the last word, a truthful one.

Tamar confronted Judah with the symbols of his authority and identity—his seal, cord, and staff—and with a message that stated she was with child by the man to whom these items belonged. He could not deny his actions or denounce what had happened. He had been willing to put Tamar to death for playing the whore, he who had negotiated the deal and enjoyed the pleasure. Judah condemned in Tamar what he excused in himself.

The truth with which Tamar confronted Judah caught him completely off balance, but the law clearly stated that if a man had sexual intercourse with a betrothed woman, a kinsman's wife, or a daughter-in-law, both the man and the woman should be put to death (Lev. 18:20; 20:12; Deut. 22:23). According to the law, Judah was guiltier than Tamar. But as judge and jury, he made another quick decision. An exception should be made in this case since he had in fact fulfilled the levirate obligation by giving Tamar the child to which she was entitled. Tamar's disclosure of Judah's paternity overturned the death sentence and consummated the levirate obligation.

Faced with the truth and exposed for his action, Judah acknowledged his irresponsibility. For the first time in the stories of Joseph and Tamar, Judah showed himself to have a heart and a conscience. Perhaps he saw Tamar for the first time, not as someone cursed by the LORD but blessed. The one thing Judah had failed to give her through the levirate law had now been provided by the LORD. Through her, Judah knew his lineage would continue. Exonerating Tamar of all guilt, Judah publicly confessed: "She is more in the right than I, since I did not give her to my son Shelah." Although the custom prohibited Judah from marrying Tamar (and also probably Shelah, for Tamar had been with his father), his words of repentance restored her to life within the tribe and gave her a place of security in the extended family. Tamar became a mother, if not a wife, and Judah claimed her twin sons as legally his own. In the end Tamar received recognition for her righteousness in pursuing fulfillment of the levirate law, and Judah was not condemned for impeding it. Instead of bringing disgrace and death into a critical situation, Tamar brought new life and hope.

We may only hope Judah genuinely repented of his treatment of Tamar. His unfaithfulness in keeping the levirate law had threatened to nullify the LORD's promise to Abraham of great posterity. Yet that promise, as well as Judah's continued posterity, had been restored by Tamar, a Canaanite woman of great initiative and vision. Perhaps Judah realized that Tamar showed more loyalty to his LORD, his name, and his tribe than he had. Out of respect for Tamar's righteousness and her deep faith in the Hebrew LORD, Judah may have given her a place of honor in the tribe and blessed her for his offspring-to-be.

At the time of Tamar's delivery, it was discovered that she was bearing twins, an event that marked a woman as a special matriarch within the tribe. The twins in Tamar's womb signaled the LORD's favor and activity on her behalf. During an unusual delivery, a crimson cord was tied to the wrist of Zerah to mark the firstborn, yet the second twin in the birth order pushed through first. He was named Perez, "a break in the wall, one who pushes through, or a breach," and was like his mother in this respect. Tamar appeared to be second in everything as far as Judah and his sons were concerned. Yet she made a break in the wall of the patriarchal system that sought to hold her back, and she pushed through the levirate law to receive what rightfully belonged to her. Refusing to be put aside, she made a place for herself in the tribe of Judah and in the memory of Israel and all Christendom. Continued through the lineage of Perez, she is remembered as the mother of Judah's twin sons and a female ancestor of King David and Jesus the Messiah.

With little political and economic power and authority, Tamar played a critical role at this turning point in Hebrew history. Tamar discerned no separation between her personal fulfillment and the fulfillment of the LORD's promises. She created transition and marked transformation. Partly due to her righteousness, Judah's tribe flourished and rose to be the most powerful of all Israel's tribes. From Judah all Judaism takes its name.

Tamar the "date palm" did indeed bear the sweetest fruit in the birth of her twin sons. For persons then and now who find themselves in impossible and unsettling situations, Tamar remains an ensign of courage. Like the stately palm tree, she stands as a witness to the Lord's assurance that wrongs can be made right.

Her-story Embedded in History

Tamar's her-story is so deeply embedded in the ancestral history of the Hebrews and the Joseph story that even with biblical study and research, gaps and unresolved relationships still remain. The violent and cruel act of Jacob's sons against Joseph, their youngest brother, alerts us to a complete breakdown of the great patriarch's family. This patriarchal tribe had always been a family divided by envy and deception. Remember how Jacob stole Esau's birthright? Remember the trickery of Laban, Jacob's father-in-law, and Jacob's eventual marriage to two sisters at the same time? Remember how

Rachel, one of Jacob's wives, stole her father's teraphim, the household idol, and then lied about stealing it? If your memory is unclear, take time to read the chapters just before Genesis 38. Soap operas do not get any better than these stories! With this heritage, is it any wonder that this son of Jacob and the patriarch in Tamar's story was self-serving and deceptive? The action of Joseph's brothers as they sold him into slavery left little possibility for reconciliation, and Judah left his father's tribe. At this point Tamar's multilayered story of intrigue begins.

Tamar's story is often interpreted as an interruption, an intrusion, a detour on the way to a more important story: a her-story versus a his-story. Its placement between other his-stories of fraud, treachery, and deceit tempts us to label it as another story of deception instigated by a female trickster. Such labeling would do a grave injustice to Tamar and her faithfulness. If we could read the story from Tamar's perspective, we might find an emphasis on relationships and consequences not present in the biblical text.

At the conclusion of Tamar's her-story, the Joseph story continues. From slavery Joseph rapidly had risen to power, becoming second in command only to Pharaoh. Jacob, along with his sons and their children and wives, sojourns to Egypt. The number included Judah's sons, Shelah, Perez, Zerah, and Perez's sons. (Perez and Zerah were Judah's twin sons by Tamar.) Since Tamar was not married to Judah or Shelah, it is uncertain whether she went to Egypt with the rest of Judah's family.

Some scholars suggest that the placement of the story of Tamar and Judah contrasts Joseph's righteousness and commitment to the LORD with Judah's shameless self-interest, deception, and mistreatment of others. That perspective overlooks the important role Tamar played in successfully ensuring the continuance of Judah's tribe when the tribe's future was threatened. Other commentators believe that when Judah's tribe rose to prominence as the forebear of King David, it became important to record its history and preserve its tradition. If this is the case, we must remember that the tribe's rise to prominence came about partly because Tamar birthed a powerful tribe into existence. Regardless of the placement of Tamar's story in the ancestral history of the patriarchs, the rather sparse and measured language in Genesis 38 records the establishment of the tribe of Judah and the important family of Perez. Perhaps her story also marks the moral maturation of Judah due to his confrontation and reconciliation with Tamar, after which he finally becomes the patriarch the LORD had called him to be.

Tamar's her-story should be read and interpreted in the period, context, and history of the Near East. The culture and history of the early Hebrews were never static but always in a state of fluidity, spanning hundreds of years before the Israelite monarchies when kings ruled (1000–586 B.C.E.). Swirling all around and deeply embedded in the ancestral history of the Hebrews were the ancient god and goddess religions, which sometimes offered more opportunities for women. Into this culture Tamar was born and from it she came as the daughter-in-law of Judah. Thus Tamar's story should not be torn from the fabric of her culture, which surely must have affected her relationships in the patriarchy of Judah's tribe and stoked the fires of her passion in seeking what was rightfully hers. While she married into a Hebrew tribe and may have become a Yahwist convert, she came from the dust of Canaan, her feet were rooted in its earth. To remember Tamar is to remember also her heritage.

Tamar and Judah lived during the settlement stage in the premonarchical period before Israel's nationhood. The people were known only as "the Hebrews." The tribal patriarch was *the* authority, determining the fate of every member of his tribe, especially

the women—those born into it and those married into it. The
women ensured the continuation of the tribe's name after the
patriarch's death. The begetter of many descendants, the patriarch
enforced the customs and traditions kept by all Twelve Tribes.

Hebrew laws and moral codes, unrecorded for centuries, passed
orally from tribe to tribe and from father to son. While situations
described in the narratives do not always correspond to and uphold
the exact keeping of the laws as recorded, they do indicate that the
laws at least were known. In some cases the laws and traditions
were ignored or exceptions made, particularly with regard to the
decree against intermarriages. According to the pious priests who
compiled and edited the laws at a much later date than the Tamar
story, intermarriage with non-Hebrews threatened the existence of
the chosen people as much as battles for the conquest of Canaan
or the exile into Egypt. The covenant with the LORD to remain
pure required absolute obedience if the Hebrews were to remain
the LORD's holy people. Intermarriage, an act of disobedience that
broke the holiness code (Deut. 7:1-6), polluted the pure bloodline
of the Hebrews.

On a contrary note, the Bible does record that some prominent men (Abraham, Jacob, and Moses, for example) married outside the Israelite family with the LORD's continued blessing. Such
intermarriages, connected too closely to Israel's history to be
ignored or criticized, forced the first scribes of the early written
records, and now us, to hold in tension two very different realities
of Hebrew intermarriage. The first reality is that the LORD accom-
modated intermarriage and used it to bless the tribes with great
posterity that made them into a mighty nation. The second reality
is that the same LORD abhorred intermarriage and used it as a reason for genocide and destruction.

Since property passed from father to son, the Hebrews created laws and customs to assure absolute knowledge of paternity. The maintenance of the patrilineal system kept all property in the tribe. Within the tribes virginity was demanded of all women (but not men) until marriage, and after marriage total fidelity. Sexual intimacy outside the bounds of marriage or the levirate bond was sinful and unlawful for women because it went against the LORD's decree. The sentence for a young virgin, a betrothed virgin, or a married woman for disobeying the law was the same—death by stoning or burning (Deut. 22:13-27). Though the levirate law existed primarily for the purpose of keeping inheritance and property within the tribe, it served as a way to control a woman's sexual encounters and ascertain a man's paternity.

Hebrew laws reflected a code of morality, but they also supported a political and economic strategy that expedited the tribes' takeover of land and property. As long as god and goddess societies with fewer restrictions on sexual contact coexisted with the Hebrew patriarchal society, paternity and the inheritance of property were threatened and could not be guaranteed.

Because the development and practice of the law differed among tribes throughout the ancestral history of the patriarchs, we cannot generalize about *all* Hebrew culture, the roles of *all* Hebrew women, the treatment of *all* Hebrew women, or the strict enforcement of *all* Hebrew laws. Nor can we generalize about *all* Canaanite cultures and religions. While we may be tempted to judge ancient Hebrew and Canaanite belief systems as unfit according to our Christian moral constructs, each made significant contributions to human civilization—many from which we still benefit.

Tamar, whose story was embedded in both Canaanite matriarchal her-story and Hebrew patriarchal history, was blessed by the LORD. In one of the strangest of all dysfunctional family stories, a woman of foreign bloodline and impregnated by her Hebrew father-in-law in an almost incestuous act gave birth to twin sons. Strengthened by her own sense of righteousness and justice, she protected herself, guaranteed her twins' security, and assured the survival of Judah's tribe. The Bible text records her name for all generations to remember, for Tamar was a memorable matriarch in whom the tribe of David took root and from whom the family tree of Jesus the Messiah took nourishment.

The Second Turning: Reading between the Lines

Throughout the Joseph story, clothing and personal items play a prominent symbolic role. A change of clothing signals a change in a situation or in the characters' lives. Joseph's distinctive cloak symbolized Jacob's great love and affection for this son, but it symbolized envy and strife for Joseph's brothers. With the removal of the cloak, the favorite son of a patriarch became a slave of Pharaoh in Egypt. Soaked with goat's blood to convince Jacob of Joseph's death, the cloak was a symbol of deception; for Jacob, who never recovered from the loss of his son, it became a symbol of grief. When Judah subsequently left his father's household, the cloak represented the severe disruption of relationships that could not be reconciled or restored.

For Tamar a change of clothes marked a transition in her authority and a new sense of self-identity and self-consciousness. A change of clothes became a symbol for finding her voice. Once ignored and overlooked, she donned different clothes and discovered a new visibility and presence. She discarded her widow's clothes that symbolized restriction and isolation for a veil and drape that covered her face and body. No longer was Tamar bound to any male—father or husband. The veil and drape symbolized her new freedom and choice. While both sets of clothes masked and disguised Tamar's identity, a change from one to the other signaled transformation in her readiness to do what she could to change her situation.

Judah's seal, cord, and staff—symbols of his authority and his pledge—became his undoing in Tamar's hands. They became markers for mediation, providing Tamar with a means of intervention in a father-son inheritance system that had shut her out. Where she was unwanted or uninvited, they gave her access into the "man's world" and reinstated her in the patriarch's tribe. She cleverly used their multiplicity of meaning to exact justice from Judah. While her actions did not change the levirate laws, Tamar brought about the LORD's will for the posterity of Judah's tribe.

Throughout the stories included in the ancestral history in Genesis, we find dishonesty, deception, trickery, and other kinds of actions that were contrary to the LORD's will for the Hebrew people and the future nation of Israel. However, the LORD did not condemn Tamar's actions and behavior as unrighteous but blessed them because they enabled the survival of the Hebrews. Judah confirmed her righteousness. Yet many scholars and commentators project Tamar as a pious and wise trickster, a biblical trickster who used intelligence, faith, sexuality, and perseverance in daring and outrageous ways.

As a Canaanite outsider disadvantaged and rendered powerless by the structure into which she married, Tamar employed charitable trickery to influence for good the course of both current and future events, taking into account the needs of the tribe and her understanding of the LORD's purposes. In terms of sexuality she knew that preservation of the lineage of Judah's tribe and fulfillment of the LORD's purpose required progeny; she used her sexuality to obtain the goal. Tamar tenaciously and actively pursued what rightfully belonged to her, using her resourcefulness to turn inequality into equality. Rather than upset the social stability of the tribe, her actions provided for the continuation of it, employing the patriarchal system to transcend boundaries. In a role reversal, Tamar became the power broker and covenant keeper, and Judah became the covenant breaker rendered powerless in the process.

Tamar's her-story uncovers the fragile state of the tribe's social order and the instability of those in power. The levirate law was meant in part to protect the widow, but a woman's place and status were always at risk. Her rights were precarious, and she did not control the thin line between security and victimization. In Tamar's story the line between the powerful (Judah) and the powerless (Tamar) is blurred, and the vulnerability of those in power becomes more visible. The weak become strong and the strong weak. Tamar becomes for us the messenger of an important theme in the Hebrew Bible: The LORD sides with the poor, the weak, and the oppressed.

Women's Rights Are Human Rights

Tamar's her-story is woven together around the issues of power, class, economic justice, and marginalization from the decision-making processes that governed women's rights. Then as now sex, gender, and control still form the core of every human rights issue for women. Tamar said no, and with that no Judah and his tribal structure of justice finally heard her voice. She received what was rightfully hers only after great personal cost. Tamar, our sister of long ago, stands as a steadfast emissary for women's human rights and a stalwart witness to women across the world who seek justice.

The idea of women treated as property seems a primitive concept that devalues the sacredness of individual personhood, deprecates human life, and dehumanizes both women and men. Yet women throughout the world live in situations that differ little from what we know about Tamar. In some cultures a woman is still considered a man's possession and property. Whatever the woman does or does not do reflects on his honor. As with Tamar, the woman is assumed guilty and is often the first to be blamed and punished.

Many women and young girls in some areas of the world live in fear of "suspected immorality," for in a complex code that sanctions the ancient tradition of honor killings, a man may kill a female relative for actual or suspected sexual activity that occurs without his approval. Women in this situation have no way of knowing what behavior will trigger their death sentence. The practice of honor killings, while not supported by religious law, traditionally obligates a man to kill the woman if he even *suspects* her of immorality. Otherwise the rest of his tribe will despise him.

Hundreds of women are killed every year in countries where honor crimes are upheld because male relatives believe the woman has somehow stained the family name and brought shame to the tribe. Honor killings are more frequent in rural and remote areas where women remain economically dependent on men and where the patriarchs and elders of the tribal villages administer justice. If and when a murderer is brought to trial, he frequently goes unpunished or is let go with only a light sentence. He is often treated as a celebrity or hero by the villagers.

Families evidence little or no concern about maintaining the honor or dignity of women in honor killings. In cases investigated by the United Nations, 90 percent of the victims were killed by or on orders from their families. We have no official tally of honor killings, but justice is not served nor the human rights of women protected in a culture where women's lives count for so little. Exactly

Lest we feel too smug about "civilized" Western attitudes, we should be disturbed by the pandemic violence perpetuated against women in the form of domestic abuse, battering, and killing. According to the Federal Bureau of Investigation (FBI), every year approximately 1,400 women are assaulted and killed in the United States by their husbands or boyfriends. Based on statistics as reported by the FBI, the number of women who have been murdered by their intimate partners is greater than the number of soldiers killed in the Vietnam War. Although 572,000 cases of domestic battering are officially reported each year, the Justice Department and FBI conservatively estimate that between two and four million women of all races and classes are assaulted and battered each year.

Crimes against some women are crimes against all women. Change will come about when courageous women and men say no to the evils that continue to dehumanize and oppress much of the world's female population. International human rights organizations and rescue committees, centers for legal assistance and aid, shelters and health stations, lawyers and activists throughout the world, religious bodies and ordinary citizens are called to join forces to ensure that every woman's rights are honored and respected.

To break the chains of injustice and tyranny, we must become like Tamar and refuse to be refused. She is our touchstone, our archetype of justice and of redeeming and transforming righteousness. As intercessors we must remain in the struggle with our sisters in small tribes and remote villages, in cities and overpopulated megalopolises throughout the world until all women can freely choose their own individual sacred destiny.

Ponderings

Please take time to reflect on and ponder what you have read and studied in this chapter. The following questions and comments are intended to assist you. They may serve as discussion starters for group study, or they may be sources for contemplation and examination for individual use. Perhaps they will prompt further study and/or action. Through them you hopefully will bring forward the multifaceted meanings and implications of this chapter for living in our day and time.

1. In our world many women on the "underside" of society are victimized, latter-day Tamars. They remain invisible and without voice. Like Judah, we make assumptions about them and pronounce them guilty before knowing the facts. We do not want them too close for fear of what they might bring upon us and those we love. We do not want to hear the claims they make upon our time and energy as they seek, in the name of justice, to redress the wrongs done to them. Our indifference can sentence these unnamed women to many kinds of deaths. Judah said to Tamar, "Remain a widow in your father's house until...." We speak similar messages to the Tamars throughout the world when we say, "Remain in your housing project infested with rats and drug dealers until.... Remain hidden away and silent in women's shelters for victims of domestic violence until.... Remain in prisons and live in fear of those who are supposed to protect you until.... Remain in terror of brutal police who have murdered your loved ones until.... Remain in rape camps and suffer through it until.... Remain in the mental hospital until.... Remain homeless and prostitute yourself to support your children until.... Remain in the closet hiding your sexual orientation until.... Remain in poverty, hunger, and unsanitary conditions until...."

- What must the Tamars of our world do and say that will finally cause us to see and hear them?

- What must the Tamars of our world finally do that will cause us to confess, "She is more in the right than we are; she is more righteous than we are"? And after the confession, what will we do? What will you do?

2. Biblical scholars and commentators assume that a man recorded Tamar's her-story.

   - How might the narrative have differed if written by a woman? Why?

   - If you had the opportunity, how would you tell the story? How would you portray Judah, Er, and Onan? What more would Tamar communicate about her feelings? How would you portray Tamar?

   - If Tamar told her story, what new insights do you think she might share?

   - Of all the characters in the story, whom would you most like to interview if given the opportunity? Why?

3. Tamar's clothes signified her identity and place in the culture to which she belonged. By changing clothes she called attention to the different social and religious functions of attire. The multiple connotations of garments became an expression of her desires and goals, a disguise to serve her own interest and purpose, and a mediating device for justice. Using garments Tamar redefined herself and successfully claimed a place for herself in a man's world. In a sense Tamar's clothes remade the woman!

   - How do women today use clothing or accessories to negotiate a "man's world"? to express their desires and goals? to get what they want and deserve? to disguise? to engender authority and respect? to redefine themselves?

4. Tamar found herself at a crossroads at the border between Enaim (a place for "the opening of the eyes") and Timnah ("on the way to a reckoning"). She had to make important decisions about remaining in her current situation or moving into an unknown future. She knew the limits of her present existence. She knew her place. There were certain comfort and security in its familiarity. But to remain where she was meant a continued slow death of all her dreams and of who she knew herself to be. True, she had to confront Judah, the external source of her dilemma. But she also had to confront her spirit from which she received her internal sense of value and worth. Her eyes were opened, and she found herself on the way to a reckoning. To be alive was to be in transition. A new beginning meant that something of the old must die.

   • When "the opening of the eyes" has happened to you and you are "on the way to a reckoning," how do you most often approach this time of discernment?

   • When you find yourself in transition at a crossroads how do you perceive the transition?

   • What encourages you to step across familiar boundaries into an unknown place of vulnerability and risk? What or whom must you confront before you can move on? How does your faith empower you when moving through times of transition?

5. Let me point to some of our societal attitudes that may be rooted in the ancient Hebrew culture into which Tamar married. It remains part of some wedding ceremonies that the father of the bride "gives" his daughter to another man. When a woman marries, the prevailing cultural attitude expects her to take on the man's paternal name as her primary identity. Children born to a married couple usually take the last name of the

father to ensure patrilineal descent. The debate about who should control a woman's body continues from the pulpit and the judicial bench. A large segment of the population understands that a woman's first responsibility in helping create a strong family is to bear children and to stay home while raising them. Property ownership and inheritance rights in some states are not favorable to women.

• In what ways does this assessment of some of the early Hebrew contributions to our culture's moral and ethical traditions seem fair or unfair? With which do you agree, and why?

6. You have become acquainted with Tamar, one of your ancient foremothers, in this chapter. Given the opportunity to read between the lines and reflect about the silences in the text, perhaps Tamar's her-story brought closer to your attention circumstances of some women throughout the world or perhaps someone you know. You may have seen some of yourself in this faithful and courageous female ancestor of Jesus.

• What impact has this study of Tamar had on your self-understanding?

• How do you think Tamar would respond to your assessment?

• What will you do with your response?

CHAPTER THREE

RAHAB

A Woman Who Made Faith Work

Before reading the chapter, take time to remember as much as you can about Rahab's story in the Bible. Recall all the details you can about who she was, her description, her relationships, and when and where she lived. Then read Joshua 2:1-24; 6:17-25; Hebrews 11:31; James 2:24-25; and Matthew 1:5*a*.

Locating the Story in the Bible

The first five books of the Hebrew Bible have pointed the Hebrews forward to the promised land of Canaan. In a real sense the book of Joshua represents the fulfillment of all that has gone before. As the account of Israel's genesis concludes, the Deuteronomistic writers begin the history and stories about the entry into and conquest of the Promised Land. The LORD gives Joshua no further laws. The people have all the laws necessary to continue to be the LORD's chosen ones. They are simply to obey the laws Moses has already made part of the oral tradition. If obedience to the cleanliness and holiness laws is kept and the chosen people remain pure, the LORD will secure their success. This obedience proves to be a big "if," since the Israelites have frequent amnesia. A challenge to obey and a promise of punishment for disobedience persist throughout the

Deuteronomistic history as recorded in the books of Deuteronomy through Second Kings.

During the time of Rahab's her-story, the people called Hebrews had a loose connection through a political network of clans and tribes that formed an extended family (Josh. 7:14). Individual tribes claimed a common ancestor, and a strong bond of loyalty existed within each tribe. The oath of loyalty was most fierce and passionate among the strongest tribes. The book of Joshua follows the Hebrews, now called the Israelites, as they enter the Promised Land. The recording of a new identity gives us a clue about the development of the Hebrew people. Not yet recognized as a nation by those who already occupy Canaan, Israel is evolving a distinct ethnic and religious identity with which to be reckoned.

We cannot consider the book of Joshua a historical account of what happened during the entry and conquest of the Promised Land. The idea of historical objectivity did not exist for the Deuteronomistic writers, for whom history served a different purpose. Their concern centered around religious truth rather than objective truth, around a theological perspective rather than a chronological account. They looked backward to explain what had gone wrong with the LORD's chosen people when everything should have been so right. Theological interpretation of the past helped them understand the Israelites' present situation. They edited and constructed an Israelite history that fulfilled what they perceived the LORD had willed and promised. Obedience resulted in the LORD's favor; disobedience brought chaos and destruction.

Writing not as an eyewitness to the battle of Jericho but from imagination and oral tradition, the writer of the book of Joshua wrote about a time quite different from his own. The writer interpreted the LORD's past work in terms of his own faith and present context. One critical historical issue faced by biblical scholars is the fact that the city of Jericho evidently did not exist at the time the story was written, which makes the writer's theological construct even more a matter of faith and conviction about the LORD's promise. Faith then was the motive for this historian, not fact or fiction. The writer intended to establish a faithful testimony about God's divine victory independent of human might. From the writer's perspective the Israelites needed only to keep the LORD's commandments, hold fast to the LORD with heart and soul, and follow the holy war regulations of destruction.

The Deuteronomistic writers used older traditions, legends, folktales, poetry, hymns, and revered personages from the past to introduce new moral and political ideas. The difficulty in reading Joshua comes in isolating these different literary types from what may have been historical reality. The Deuteronomistic writers held a common belief that the LORD had prepared a land for the LORD's covenant people and that the LORD's will shaped all that had happened to the Israelites.

The recorders interpreted historical events (part of the Israelites' memory) through the lens of this theology, sometimes inflating or bending historical events to serve their strict theology. The intent of the recorded Mosaic laws, for example, from the age of the patriarchs through the exodus from Egypt often differed from the actual practices of the Hebrews and Israelites.

No matter the interpretation, the book of Joshua does have historical merit. It gives the reader a sense of the struggles that confronted the Hebrews as wilderness wanderers and settlers in Canaan. As they grew into a corporate consciousness of their vocation and unity as the chosen people of the LORD, their clans and tribes began to build alliances, sharing common religious traditions and political interests. Settled in a homeland, they instituted and celebrated common pilgrimages and festivals held at specified "shrines" to honor the LORD and to give thanks for the gracious deeds and gifts of the LORD to Israel. From these pilgrimages and festivals there developed the concept of the LORD as King of Israel, and the history of the Israelites as a nation began to emerge.

The date of the entry of the Israelites into the land of Canaan is thought to have occurred in the thirteenth century about 1250 to 1200 B.C.E. during the late Bronze Age, but the date cannot be verified with complete historical accuracy. Contradictory evidence precludes a widely held conclusion about the actual taking of the land. One perspective suggests that by the time Moses died and Joshua assumed leadership, the Twelve Tribes had merged into a defined confederation that attacked Jericho and entered Canaan in one swooping movement. Another holds that over time and through tribal battles with the Canaanites, the Israelites gradually moved into Canaan, occupying the hill country and taking over the land. Following the establishment of a common identity under the rule of judges and in response to the need for a more centralized government, the kingships of Saul, and then David and Solomon, came about. Given the lack of historical material beyond the biblical text and insubstantial archaeological evidence, the various stages of Israel's entry into and conquest of Canaan may never be known. But we read Rahab's story in the first part of the book of Joshua, which recounts a swooping takeover of Canaan by Joshua and the Israelites.

Rahab's story is probably a fragment of a much older remembered tradition. When isolated from the surrounding story of Jericho's fall, it can be analyzed and understood as a tradition in its own right. Rahab's her-story uses the biblical motif of the "spy story" (Num. 13–14; Josh. 7:2-5; Judg. 1:22-26; 18:2-11; 2 Sam. 17:17-22). Usually the spies (male) enter a hostile environment and promise salvation to those in a community deemed least worthy of the LORD's salvation. As the spies prepare to follow through on the promised destruction, they exhibit courage, heroics, and resource-fulness. The female characters, shadowed and undefined, remain uninvolved in the spies' achievements.

Rahab's her-story has a different twist than other biblical spy stories. Here an unknown woman of questionable reputation holds the "keys to the city" and the passage for the spies and all Israel to the Promised Land. This spy story is a woman's story. Though we may wonder how spies managed to get into Jericho and go unde-tected by the king until they were at Rahab's house, the writer knew that readers would delight in the bumbling and stumbling action of the enemy king's patrol rushing off in the wrong direction as the Israelite spies escape down the outer walls of the city. What is par-ticularly unusual about this story is that the spies are eclipsed in knowledge and courage by a Canaanite prostitute. As the passive spies await rescue, Rahab initiates action and with little difficulty fools everyone.

The Deuteronomistic writers favored the literary form of declam-atory speech, usually credited to an important Israelite leader. In the book of Joshua, Rahab, a foreign woman and a prostitute, speaks with authority (Josh. 2:9-11). The writer perceives Rahab as a deci-sive and heroic figure, key to the Israelites' entrance into Canaan and their successful military campaign against the Canaanites. We get the strong impression that the Israelites revered this woman.

Joshua 2:1-24 presents Rahab as a primary character. In a later chapter she does not speak, but her name is mentioned three times (Josh. 6:17-25). While not a figure in the New Testament, she is remembered three times in its pages. The early Christian commu-nity acknowledged her obedience and faithfulness. Hebrews 11:31 tells us that "by faith Rahab the prostitute did not perish with those who were disobedient, because she had received the spies in peace." (Sarah and Rahab are the only women named in the long roll call of the faithful recorded in Hebrews.) James 2:24-25 promotes Rahab

JAMES

as a model of obedience: "a person is justified by works and not by
faith alone. Likewise, was not Rahab the prostitute also justified by
works when she welcomed the messengers and sent them out by
another road?" A prostitute by profession, Rahab is honored as
one justified by her works of faith. Her decisive action opened the
way to the Promised Land for the Israelites. Matthew 1:5-8 names
Rahab as one of the female ancestors of Jesus the Messiah.

Ask a Question—Get a Story

Why does the saving activity of the LORD's work in settling the
Israelites in the Promised Land begin at the house of a Jericho
prostitute? What kind of woman would betray her own king and
city to strangers who were the enemy? Was Rahab an opportunist
who took advantage of the Israelite spies in order to save her life
and all that belonged to her? Or can we decipher her action as
faithfulness that rested securely in a God she knew only by reputation? Dare we open our eyes and our hearts wide enough to
embrace the woman known only as Rahab the prostitute, or do we
resist Rahab's her-story because of her profession? Why would a
prostitute be honored as one of the female ancestors of Jesus?
What are we to remember about Rahab?

Rahab, a prostitute housed within the city wall of Jericho, had
a location readily available to travelers. Because of her profession,
Rahab's reputation in the city was undoubtedly questionable. Her
isolation from the community that shunned her actually allowed
the Israelite spies easy access to her. (No honorable Canaanite
woman would meet alone with strange men.) But Rahab the prostitute did not behave as we might have expected. Compassionate
and vulnerable, she confessed to the spies her faith in the Israelites'
LORD, who had been with the Israelites and had led them to victory in battles. Convinced that their LORD was the only God in

heaven above and on earth below, she felt certain that the Israelites would conquer Canaan. This conviction gave her the courage to negotiate safety for herself and her family and to save them from death. Heeding the warning of the spies, she fastened a crimson cord in her window, a signal for the Israelite soldiers to preserve all gathered in her house, saving them from destruction.

Rahab saw an imminent future for Israel in the land of Canaan that perhaps neither her king nor Joshua and his spies saw as clearly. In her vision the LORD had already taken the land and given it to the Israelites. Her faith moved her to take action, and she became an important player in the fulfillment of the LORD's plan for Israel's victory in Canaan. Rahab's faith and surprising discernment enabled her to act on the unproved loyalty of Israelite spies. She provided hospitality, hid them, and faithfully fulfilled her oath, at the same time opening the way for the Israelites' entrance into the Promised Land. Because of Rahab's faithfulness Joshua spared her and her whole family, who eventually settled permanently among the Israelites. Rahab was honored by generations of Israelites as a woman of faith whose saving work ended their wandering in the wilderness and brought them "home."

A woman of intellectual dexterity and wit, Rahab used the difficulty of the present moment to her advantage, envisioning a better future for herself, her family, and all of Israel. She allowed the walls of the familiar to collapse around her, exposing herself to an uncertain future and an unknown God. Rahab may have spun thread and made linen because stalks of flax were spread out to dry on her roof. Perhaps in helping the spies, Rahab seized an opportunity to spin something new into existence. With prophetic resolve she spun together strands of faith, loyalty, and action, and the fabric of Israel and Canaan changed forever.

As we deal kindly with Rahab the prostitute, perhaps we too will experience her saving actions. If we choose to step from behind the walls that separate us and let them crumble around our preconceptions of who she was, Rahab may yet extend her hand of hospitality and open for us the way to a new and uncharted promised land where we will finally find ourselves at "home."

The First Turning: Remembering

Canaanite cities were scattered across the lowlands and along the coastal plains of the Great Sea. Each city was a kingdom with its own ruler, trained military personnel, business and commerce, education, religious temples, and stratums of social and economic class, including peasants who lived in severe poverty and under oppressive landlords. The plentiful water and fruitful agricultural production of these independent cities tucked inside sturdy walls made them self-contained units. Canaanite civilization and technology were advanced and Canaanite artistry and handiwork highly refined.

Cities such as Jericho had existed for at least six centuries before Joshua appeared on the scene. The economic power held tightly in the grip of the king and his elite citizenry meant the less privileged population, especially the peasants, suffered extreme misfortune. Social unrest and political turmoil had exhausted the people. Before the arrival of Joshua and the Israelites at Shittim, which means "acacia trees," most of the city kingdoms were in a state of chaos and confusion.

The LORD's first message to Joshua encouraged the Israelites to prepare to enter the Promised Land. Joshua sent two unnamed spies across the river to look over the enemy territory, and especially to check out the city of Jericho and its defenses. The spies set out; but before attending to their mission, they went straightway to the house of a local prostitute named Rahab. Rahab's house was neither her family's nor her father's house but her own. Because she was a professional woman who operated a business establishment, it probably functioned both as her place of lodging and business.

Perhaps the spies thought they would be less conspicuous in Rahab's house. A good place to overhear talk of the men from the city and any travelers passing through, her house provided the spies with cover and access. And maybe Rahab, an outsider even in her own city, would be more considerate of other outsiders. A prostitute who would give herself to any and everyone for a price might also sell information to the spies. Yes, the decision to visit the prostitute's house was a good one but not necessarily a wise one, because the young spies did not go unnoticed by the king's patrol.

Small bands and tribes of Hebrews had wandered in Canaan for years, but with the Israelite multitude of thousands gathered across the river from Jericho, any Israelite within the walls of the city now became suspect. Not only the king but the citizens of Jericho as well found the nearby presence of a large enemy encampment, an enemy whose reputation preceded them, disturbing. Stories about the LORD of the Israelites, who led them into battle in their holy wars and miraculously saved them, had passed from Canaanite city to city. The people of Jericho had heard how the Israelites destroyed everything by the edge of their swords— men and women, young and old, animals, vegetation—when they captured a city. A thick blanket of fear smothered the city and terrorized the population.

Caught between the threat of the king's patrol and the dangerous presence of the Israelite spies, Rahab's house filled with the tension that surrounded Jericho. Accustomed to awkward situations, Rahab perhaps saw a way to work this one to her own advantage. Without hesitation, Rahab made a pivotal decision for her future and for all Israel and Canaan.

Rahab probably knew of the Israelites' encampment across the Jordan and suspected an attack on the city. A prostitute might have heard all sorts of things from her customers—perhaps even from the spies themselves. In a moment of quick assessment, Rahab reviewed the situation, calculated the risks, realized she had little chance on her own, and decided to align herself with the side she thought would win. Through years of hardship and survival, Rahab had learned that to separate herself from those in power was foolish. In this tumultuous time the Israelites held the balance of power. She would help the spies and become a traitor!

Members of the king's patrol may have frequented Rahab's establishment, exchanging favors for her services. Surely the king's patrol knew the prostitute's working rhythms. Perhaps lulled by that familiarity, they agreed to wait a few minutes before insisting that Rahab respond to the king's command to bring out the men who had entered her house. Rahab took action. Without regret or ambivalence she hid the Israelite spies, careful to display no signs of anxiety or betrayal. Speaking with conviction and passion, Rahab lied to the king's patrol.

Apparently Rahab's feigned ignorance convinced them. A prostitute did not make inquiries of those who came to enjoy her services, an amenity the members of the patrol may themselves have enjoyed. With no more questions, the king's patrol rushed off in hot pursuit of the spies. In the meantime, if the spies thought they would rest on the roof under the stars, they soon learned Rahab had something else in mind. In spite of her concern about the welfare of her family and herself and about the risk she had taken in betraying the king, she believed that the army of Jericho was no match for the Israelites. The conversation she now must have with the spies was a matter of life or death.

No longer speaking as an unknowing prostitute but with seriousness and an anxious heart, Rahab made a calculation for survival that became a revelation of faith. Rahab told the spies of the fear that gripped the city of Jericho. Because she knew the LORD of the Israelites was leading the way now and had already given the Israelites the land, Rahab then made a confession of faith about the power and majesty of their LORD. In an astounding profession of belief, she confided to the spies that the LORD their God was far greater than any of the Canaanite idols and that surely their LORD was the one and only God. While Rahab feared the actions of the warring Israelites, she clearly feared more what their LORD and God might do. With her confession of faith and her profession of belief, she became a willing intercessor on behalf of others.

Rahab's fear did not squelch her loyalty and love for her family's safety. She asked the spies to swear by the LORD their God that they would deal kindly with her and her family, whom she named one by one, delivering them from harm and death. Calculating that the spies owed her this much, she also asked for a reliable sign, a token of their promise.

The spies, dependent on Rahab's ingenuity to get them past the locked gate and out of the city safely, gave her their pledge. Rahab knew the important part the spies would play in the destiny of her family and had no recourse but to accept their promise. With this agreement, Rahab, already an intercessor on behalf of the spies, became an intercessor for her family as well. Trusting in their promise, she lowered the spies down by a rope through her window.

Current archaeological evidence indicates that a unique construction of casement walls was used during the latter part of the late Bronze Age. Although Jericho had been in ruin for years, the general characterization of this construction fits the building of Jericho's walls. A fortification was built with two parallel walls around the entire city's circumference. To strengthen the structure, cross-walls were built and filled with rock and dirt or partitioned off into separate rooms within the wall itself. This description fits well with the story and with what we know about Canaanite cities during the time the Israelites were gaining entrance to the land. The biblical text clearly states that Rahab's house was built in the actual wall itself, so the window through which she lowered the spies was on the outer side of the parallel casement walls.

Rahab did not leave the future of the spies to chance. Having seen the king's patrol take off in the direction of the Jordan, she told the spies to head for the hills in the opposite direction. But at a time when they should have been listening intently, the spies began to talk. Once on the ground and in control of their own situation, again they began to recite the conditions under which they would keep their oath to Rahab.

Sensing the danger of being discovered in conversation with Israelite spies, Rahab sealed the agreement with few words: "According to your words, so be it." With a sense of covenant, Rahab sent them away and immediately tied a crimson cord in her window as she had promised.

What kind of woman has the tenacity and inner courage to negotiate her own terms with enemy spies, making them take an oath and insisting they leave a reliable sign that they will keep it? Rahab possessed unusual spirit and strength to find a way out of such a difficult situation. The life of a prostitute had taught her to be her own woman and to take care of herself first. In her new role as an intercessor who had pledged her faith to an unfamiliar Israelite LORD, she learned to trust in something and someone greater than herself. Perhaps with the experience and acceptance of the saving grace of faith, she chose life. She could not predict the unknown and unpredictable future, but she embraced its unseen mystery and chose its promise over certain death if she remained where she was.

Surely the spies admired Rahab's refusal to be dominated

either by the king's patrol or them. Rahab had offered sound and trustworthy advice. The spies reported to Joshua Rahab's exact words. What else could they have said? That they had been in the house of a prostitute and talked only with the prostitute herself? That before they could check out Jericho, they were caught by the king's patrol? That the same prostitute planned their escape? That they had been hiding in the hill country for three days? That was not the report Joshua would expect, so they spoke Rahab's words.

Leaving Shittim and preparing for battle, Joshua and all Israel gathered on the Jericho plains near the Jordan River. Dreading the prospect of war, the population of Jericho was terror-stricken. Silence more deadly than death seeped through the walled city. At a time when everything and everyone in Jericho were suspect, the crimson cord that had hung in Rahab's window for several days drew no one's attention. Business had been slow during these tumultuous times, and passersby who noticed it probably thought Rahab was attempting to get more customers. But for Rahab the crimson cord was a visible sign of invisible hope, an assurance of a future reality she could not see. She did not know how or when it would arrive, but she believed that the spies would keep their oath and that the LORD of the Israelites would save her and her family.

In accordance with the oath the two young spies had given Rahab, Joshua told them to go to the prostitute's house and rescue her and all her kindred on the day Jericho fell to the Israelites. However, Rahab's clan were all Canaanites and idol worshipers; a collision of cultures and religions ensued, and Rahab and her family became war refugees outside the camp of Israel. Over time Rahab's family probably converted to Yahwism. The text tells us that Rahab and her family settled permanently in Israel, apparently adopted as Israelites and living among the LORD's chosen people.

We will never know why the Deuteronomistic writers included Rahab's her-story in the sacred writings of the Hebrews. Maybe they wanted to explain how a Canaanite clan could survive Jericho's destruction and live on among the Israelites. However, centuries before Rahab was remembered in the epistle of James, she had prophetically heralded the foundation of Christian living—that "faith without works is also dead" (James 2:26). Down through the ages of Jewish and Christian tradition, Rahab has shown what it means to live a life that spins together faith and works and weaves from their strands a tapestry of salvation and redemption.

Rahab experienced what all of us want to know: a faith that works. For Rahab faith involved more than words; it was anchored in action and sustained by hope. Rahab's faith saved her and her family. It ushered the LORD's covenant people into the Promised Land and made a place for her and her family in the household of Israel and in the genealogy of Jesus. For those today who seek to be faithful to God's call upon their lives, Rahab the prostitute may have lessons yet to teach us about faith that hopes and works in holy ways to redeem and restore self and others.

Her-Story Embedded in History

We cannot separate Rahab's her-story from the historical and cultural context that has been handed down to us in the book of Joshua. Delving into the Israelites' mind-set about the fate of non-Israelites and their possessions helps us better grasp the unusual nature of Rahab's rescue and survival, her subsequent life among the LORD's chosen people, and her revered status in Israel as the mother of prophets.

Rich in tradition, artistry, innovation, and myth, civilization had existed in Canaan centuries before the Israelites arrived. Plentiful water supplies and sound agricultural practices made it "a land flowing with milk and honey," but the Israelites did not yet possess it. However, through Moses the land had been promised to them as an inheritance by their LORD. Reminded that previous failures and losses had a direct relationship with their disobedience (particularly in the areas of idol worship and intermarriage among non-Israelites), Joshua demanded that his followers pledge complete obedience and fidelity to the LORD God.

Israel believed itself called to establish a radically different sovereign nation; therefore, a holy war with Jericho and the Canaanites loomed on the horizon. Rahab's premonition that Israel's LORD had already given the land to the Israelites would soon come to pass, and the mass destruction of Jericho followed. Victory in Jericho consummated the LORD's promise, confirmed Israel's identity as the LORD's covenant people, and made absolute the claim that the LORD God surpassed all Canaanite deities. Other than Rahab and her family, the fate of the other Jericho survivors is uncertain. The wonder is that Rahab trusted an enemy's oath and courageously kept her faith in the Israelite LORD, whom she proclaimed as the only God of heaven above and on earth below.

The book of Judges makes it apparent that the taking of the rest of Canaan may have been a slower process than the battle of Jericho suggests. Judges picks up with the ongoing attempts of the Israelites to conquer and take Canaan. The speed of the Israelite takeover of Canaan is not the point of Rahab's her-story. The ancient sages and rabbis honored Rahab as their threshold into the Promised Land, the prostitute of uncanny insight, a hero of faith, and a friend of Israel. They remembered her significant role in the divine victory at Jericho and the Israelites' entrance into Canaan.

The Second Turning: Reading between the Lines

It is curious that the historical writings give such a prominent place in the opening story to Rahab the prostitute. Over the ages Rahab's her-story has been censored, suppressed, or ignored. In order to soften Rahab's occupation, some ancient scholars, both Jewish and Christian, perpetuated the idea that Rahab simply served as an "innkeeper." But the biblical writer seems to preserve deliberately the sexual elements of Rahab's her-story—a common prostitute makes good with her trade.

Some of today's religious scholars, church school educators, and preachers find Rahab's profession offensive, and her story makes others uncomfortable. Many still go to great lengths to clean up the story, to make it more acceptable and fitting for Christian consumption, especially Christian youth. But labeling Rahab's her-story inappropriate or incompatible with Christian instruction misses the point. The vitality of the text comes through God's regard for Rahab, for her worthiness of God's blessing just as she was, which is a source of great hope for every one of us.

When Rahab's her-story began, she was neither an insider nor an outsider. She had no place on either side of the Israelite-Canaanite conflict. For the Israelites, Rahab did not have the right ethnicity nor did she worship the right God. Not being one of the chosen people, she did not count. For the Canaanites Rahab's profession as a common prostitute said it all. They would use her, but they would never allow her to be an insider. Even her house built in a wall, itself the boundary between the inside and the outside of Jericho, symbolized her marginalization.

Pushed aside and overlooked, Rahab perhaps experienced the divine presence in her encounter with the two young Israelite spies. Neither their bravery and righteousness nor Rahab's fear of the Israelites brought her to God. But her deep desire to find a safe haven for her family in the midst of Israel's battle with Jericho launched her leap of faith to holiness. What Rahab had heard about the power of the LORD encouraged her commitment to a future with this unknown God of the Israelites. When Rahab the prostitute felt the LORD's empowerment, her heart became holy ground and a fit dwelling place for the mysterious power and presence of the Holy One.

Tradition has assumed that Joshua and future generations knew that Rahab possessed the power and presence of God's holiness. According to rabbinic tradition, she was the ancestor of ten priests and one prophetess. Rahab's faith and her redemptive and intercessory actions of holiness identified her as one of God's own. Rahab the prostitute, an outsider, may have better understood the nature and love of God than did the insiders of the house of Israel.

In Rahab's her-story Joshua learned again what he should already have known—that God desires to save God's beloved children, that salvation is beyond human manipulation and ingenuity, and that God's grace is for all—regardless of race, nationality, or religion. The continued presence of Rahab and her family in Israel served to remind Joshua and the Israelites of the abiding truth of this universal lesson. Perhaps this message inclined the Deuteronomistic writer to place Rahab the prostitute's her-story at the beginning of the account of God's saving action.

Women's Rights Are Human Rights

With few exceptions Canaanite women in the book of Joshua were invisible victims of holy wars initiated and fought by men. Like Rahab's, the fate of Canaanite women was tied to their warriors' victory or loss in the battle of Jericho. No wonder Rahab persisted in her negotiations with the young Israelite spies; her situation, a matter of life or death, left no room for miscalculation. Had Rahab not saved the spies or made them take an oath, they would have been compelled to destroy her in battle, to devote her to destruction according to the LORD's commandment. Rahab courageously and assertively pursued freedom with wit, wile, and intelligent forethought.

While Israelite women fared better during the battle of Jericho and entrance into the Promised Land than did Canaanite women, they remained under the authority of the male head of the household. This male dominance encouraged a sense of entitlement to and possession of women. As in the time of Tamar and Judah, the fathers passed on religious traditions and educated their sons about the LORD's commandments for the chosen people. With few exceptions, property ownership and inheritance were passed on patrilineally. In the book of Joshua Israelite women were not educated about nor did they participate in the covenant between Israel and the LORD.

During this period in Israel's history, women resided in the margins of Israelite religious life and rituals, with little voice except in the domain of child rearing and household issues. Because Israel's structures of governance and administration made no place for them, the more ancient accounts and traditions seldom include women's roles. Deuteronomistic historians edited them out, but Rahab refused to be edited out. Her example encourages us to take action to right the wrongs that still exist in our global society.

In many countries women and children remain invisible victims of wars initiated and fought by men who claim their wars to be God's will. Edited out by media and political powers, women and children are most vulnerable and least protected during battle sieges; they are also the most coveted "spoils" of war. The attitude is that men who have fought hard are entitled to them. With victory comes the reality that women and girls are used sexually, raped, kidnapped, and frequently imprisoned in slave brothels or rape camps.

The crisis of civil war in Liberia is but an example of the war crimes perpetrated against women and girls across the globe. During the years of civil war in Liberia, the World Health Organization found that more than one-third of an estimated 500,000 displaced women and children were raped. This international agency's records are filled with reports on the torture and killing of girls, pregnant women, and mothers.

Victims are ashamed to take action against those who violate them, and neither the legal system nor the extended family structures supports a woman's initiative to take such action. At great risk women from the different warring factions came together and organized peace groups that helped to bring a peace—though restless and unstable—to the country of Liberia. The president of the Association of Female Lawyers of Liberia stated a universal truth that we too conveniently ignore: "When one woman suffers, all women suffer." Truthfully the suffering of one human being, whether woman, man, or child, diminishes us all.

Wars fought by the armed forces of different sides and nations expend an immense amount of energy, monies, and human lives. These situations often distract us from the other kinds of wars that destroy the human heart and do violence to the human soul: wars of politics, economics, religion, gender, domestic violence, class, race, hunger, poverty. These are only some of the conflicts that keep women and children suffering a fate not of their choosing. Standing by Rahab of long ago, their fate, like hers, is tied to winners or losers of battles.

Women and children easily are exploited or become expendable commodities of war. Relegated to the status of outsiders, their lives become barter for ammunition or other goods, subject to the whim of and for the convenience of those who have status and access to governmental, legal, military, and family decision-making mechanisms. They remain unprotected from those who feel entitled to take what they want from those they exploit. Violence to women is the most frequent expression of entitlement.

We can trace wars related to economic and territorial gain to the beginning of human history. A tragic consequence of war is often the trafficking of the human body for sexual exploitation. The biblical narratives of the Hebrew Bible and the story of Joshua include such stories. Although an ancient trade, the trafficking of women and children for the sex industry has reached an all-time high in the twenty-first century. Amnesty International reports that trafficking in human beings is one of the largest sources of profit for international organized crime. Only guns and drugs are bigger business.

A more recent form of exploitation, extensive in Asia, is sex tourism, which became common in the 1970s and has increased steadily since then. During the Vietnam War, American troops went to Bangkok for rest and recuperation breaks. This steady stream of business in the sex industry buoyed the local economy. When the war ended, the government, military, and businesses of some Asian countries began to promote and organize sex tourism as a way to keep money flowing into the economy. Organized primarily for men, packaged sex tours bring men from all over the world to cities in Asia known for their "hospitality." Sex tourism is a big-business enterprise that satisfies men and enslaves women and children, keeping them in debt, imprisoned, and in perilous health.

Information networks promoting sex tourism include magazines and books full of glossy pictures and details about women and children for men on "holiday" to do with as they like. Anything and everything goes. Child prostitution is one of the horrific aspects of the sex tourism industry. Young children are frequently labeled "virgins" because it is believed they are less likely to expose clients to AIDS.

Rahab the prostitute knew the truth about the consequences of war and the suffering of women and children who were outsiders. Portrayed as a successful prostitute of some notoriety and means, she remained a woman exploited and controlled by men.

Backed against the wall by male dominance, control, and entitlement from which escape was almost impossible, Rahab found a way to break down the walls of hostility that held her captive. Her faithful actions redeemed her and her family, and she stands before us as redeemer and friend, reminding us that women and children still suffer. When anyone suffers anywhere in the world, everyone suffers everywhere. No one is free until all are free.

Ponderings

Please take time to reflect on and ponder what you have read and studied in this chapter. The following questions and comments are intended to assist you. They may serve as discussion starters for group study, or they may be sources for contemplation and examination for individual use. Perhaps they will prompt further study and/or action. Through them you hopefully will bring forward the multifaceted meanings and implications of this chapter for living in our day and time.

1. Rahab the prostitute showed compassion and concern for her enemies, the Israelite spies, and she was rewarded for her faith and courage. However, by listening to the silences in the biblical text we may discover that Rahab's motivation was less love of neighbor and more self-interest.

    *   What do you perceive was the motivating factor behind Rahab's saving the spies and betraying her king and people? What in her-story confirms your perspective?

    *   How does having self-interest as a motive affect your view of Rahab's actions? When has self-interest rather than concern for others served a higher purpose in your own life and in the lives of others?

    *   Midrash in this chapter refers to Rahab as an intercessor on behalf of the spies and her family. What distinction do you draw between intercession and self-interest? How does that distinction help or hinder your understanding of Rahab?

2. Rahab seems to be an out-and-out liar. Yet Hebrews 11:31 holds her up as a model of obedience, telling us that "by faith Rahab the prostitute did not perish with those who were disobedient, because she had received the spies in peace."

- Why do you believe Rahab is presented as a model of faith? Which of her characteristics do you find most appealing?

- In what instances would you find it acceptable and more faithful to lie rather than to tell the truth?

- If you found yourself in a situation like Rahab's, how would you decide about the future? What action would you take on behalf of yourself and those you love?

3. Some scholars suggest that the lesson learned from the conquest of Jericho is not the glorification of mass destruction and war but the importance of obedience.

- What historical or religious events based in blind obedience to a god or to a perceived divine cause have perpetuated evil?

- What difference do you see between this unquestioning obedience and Israel's obedience to the Lord?

- When have you known good to come from evil, redemption from destruction?

- What lessons about faith and obedience have you learned from the biblical account of Israel's conquest of the Promised Land? How does your learning include Rahab's story?

4. In spite of our resistance to its warlike brutality, the book of Joshua brings us face-to-face with many issues that Rahab witnessed and that we witness in the world—issues of war, territorial claims, nationalism, racism, pluralism, and exclusivisms of every kind. To read Rahab's story thoughtfully means we cannot escape our culpability in implicitly perpetuating some of the very things we abhor in the biblical story.

- How can Christians understand and interpret God's justice and mercy in a diverse and deeply divided world community that often views Christianity as exclusive and closed?

- What boundaries do you place on God's justice and mercy? Where would you place Rahab with regard to your boundaries?

- What price is paid when members of one nation, race, culture, religion, class, or caste believe they are most favored by the God of their choosing?

5. Abuse of women, young girls, and children seems to be a systemic issue in many cultures throughout the world, including industrialized nations like the United States of America.

   - What do you think is the genesis of this entrenched attitude that condones violence to women?

   - With Rahab's example of willingness to risk without guarantee, what can women do to claim more completely the right to make choices that lead to a life free from fear?

   - What can women who have freedom of speech and assembly do to initiate actions of social and political change on behalf of women, young girls, and children who have little voice and few freedoms? What can you do?

6. One way to get involved in stopping violence aimed at children and young girls is to contact ECPAT (End Child Prostitution in Asian Tourism). Promoting responsible political and social opportunities for involvement, this international agency advocates for the rights and welfare of children by informing and raising public awareness about the consequences of pedophiliac activity perpetrated by sex tourism in Asia. ECPAT has a branch office in the United States that is administered by the United States National Council of Churches at 475 Riverside Drive, Room 620, New York, NY 10115. The Asian address is P. O. Box 178, Klong-chan, Bangkok 10240, Thailand.

- How do you feel about an agency such as ECPAT and the possibility it offers for involvement?

- How does ECPAT's stance against child prostitution encourage you to develop greater awareness of the rights and welfare of the world's children?

- What would it take for you to become an intercessor for others as did Rahab?

7. Rahab the prostitute has been your companion in this chapter. Unlike the trafficking of human beings who are coerced or victimized, Rahab's profession presumably was chosen, making her inclusion in the genealogy of Jesus all the more surprising. Rahab made a way for the Israelites, herself, and her family where there was no way. Unknowingly she prepared a way for the birth of Jesus the Messiah.

- What impact has this study of Rahab had on your self-understanding?

- How are you like or unlike Rahab?

- How do you think Rahab would respond to your assessment? What will you do with your response?

CHAPTER FOUR

RUTH

A Woman Who Loved the Enemy

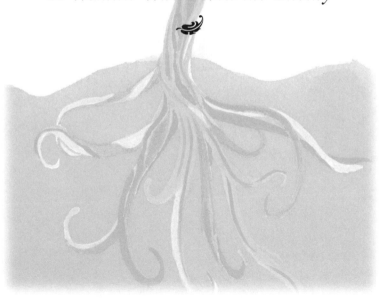

BEFORE READING the chapter, take time to remember as much as you can about Ruth's story in the Bible. Recall all the details you can about who she was, her description, her relationships, and when and where she lived. Then read the entire book of Ruth (85 verses) in the Hebrew Bible and Matthew 1:5*b*.

The story of Ruth is the longest of the narratives of the four female ancestors of Jesus. The book of Ruth consists of only 85 verses. Direct dialogue between the characters, given to 55 verses, weaves many textures and layers into the fabric of Ruth's her-story. Its woof and warp crisscross to make an intricate and complex design. Given this complexity, it will take longer to unravel the twisted threads of relationships and customs in their varied meanings and contexts.

Locating the Story in the Bible

The book of Ruth is one of two books in the entire Bible that bear a woman's name; the other is the book of Esther. The Hebrew Bible contains both. While the her-stories of Tamar and Rahab are part of a long narrative that begins in Genesis and continues through Joshua, the short narrative of Ruth's her-story stands alone and does not necessarily depend on other books in the Hebrew Bible for meaning or interpretation. The Tamar and Rahab narratives are part of a focus on the development of a national and religious identity within the Israelite clans and tribes, but in Ruth the focus is on one single family unit and its determination to stay together.

Ruth's her-story is not about war and death or strategies to gain land and goods through betrayal and violence. The book of Ruth is about inclusion, about the qualities that bind a family together across boundary lines of ethnicity and religion. It is about life and love—about kindness, loyalty, and commitment to the other and to Israel's LORD. This book also examines the LORD's loving-kindness (*chesed*) and fidelity to those who extend loving-kindness to one another. With its complex and layered meanings, the book of Ruth is a classic story unlike any other in the biblical texts. While there may have been many reasons for writing the book, perhaps the best was simply to tell a story about peace and goodwill in a climate of treachery and death.

Although actually written at a later date, the story that unfolds in Ruth takes place during the period of Israel's judges and before the monarchy of King David. With this placement the book of Ruth is part of the Deuteronomistic history and serves as a link between the days of the judges and the beginning of Israel's monarchy. Within a movement that stretches from the ancients to the kings, the book of Ruth arcs across time and brings together that which has been and is yet to come in a manner both gentle and steadfast, like the woman for whom this book is named.

Scholars still debate the date of the writing of Ruth. The story itself sets the date squarely during the period of the judges (twelfth and eleventh centuries B.C.E.), but some biblical scholars and commentators believe Ruth was written during or after the exile from Babylon (sixth or fifth centuries B.C.E. or later). Strong nationalistic tendencies and the insistence on racial purity through the purging of outsiders usually occurred during times of mistreatment of the Israelites by foreigners. Clear boundaries between "us" and "others" became an important issue in the identity of the Israelite community. Such was the situation during the times of Ezra and Nehemiah. If written during this period, the book of Ruth may have been intended to counter the insensitive decrees of Ezra and Nehemiah against intermarriage and their prescriptive orders for the Israelites to get rid of all non-Israelite wives and children (Ezra 9–10 and Neh. 10:30; 13:23-27).

Reading the book of Ruth as a counter to the purging of outsiders and to the strong nationalism of Ezra and Nehemiah moves the reader away from the prevailing idea of the LORD as an avenging warrior God, a gatekeeper who despises and abhors non-Israelites. Indeed the story of Ruth affirms that the LORD accepts faithful foreigners and outsiders and welcomes them into the household of Israel. It may have served as a model to the Israelites for the acceptance of foreigners, including non-Israelite women, as the right and godly thing to do.

Some scholars believe the book of Ruth is based on an older oral tradition or a folktale from an earlier time. Scholars agree that it might have been written before the development of Israel's bitter enmity toward Moab and the Moabites (Deut. 23:3-6) and edited at yet a later time. If the book was written after the LORD's injunctions against the Moabites recorded in Deuteronomy, the writer may have written it during one of the peaceful periods when Moabites and Israelites crossed each other's borders with impunity.

Before David became king, he had friendly, perhaps even familial, connections with Moab. While he hid from Saul in a cave, David sent his parents for safe harbor to Moab where they lived as long as David remained in hiding (1 Sam. 22:3-4). Moabite blood flowed in David's veins through the mother roots of Ruth. The genealogy that concludes the book of Ruth focuses on David and provides important lineage information that legitimizes his kingship for Hebrew readers.

Scholars disagree about the genealogy with which the book of Ruth ends. Some believe an editor added it later. Others argue that since the books of Samuel had failed to record David's ancestry, the writer attempts to do so in this closing genealogy. Many biblical scholars believe the genealogy is as old as the inclusion of the book of Ruth in the narratives from Genesis through Second Kings. The importance of the genealogy cannot be diminished, because it places the characters in the book of Ruth and those who came before and after within the Hebrew tradition where they will be remembered. The genealogy begins with Perez, the son of Judah by Tamar, and ends nine generations later with David.

Ruth's her-story includes David's genealogy, but she also is connected to Elimelech whose family tree begins the book of Ruth. Elimelech and his heirs from the ancient clan of the Ephrathites settled in Bethlehem before the story about Ruth takes place. The name Ephrathite probably comes from a root word that means "fruitful, productive, or fertile." Interestingly, the clan took its name from the mother of the clan, Ephrath (perhaps the first hint of the primary role women will play in Ruth's her-story.)

Elimelech and his family apparently were known for their productivity and fruitfulness in Bethlehem, but in Moab they found only barrenness and death. Elimelech, Naomi's husband, and her two sons, Chilion and Mahlon, died one after the other and left no seed, no fruit, no children. Mahlon was Ruth's husband. The Elimelech genealogy at the beginning of the book balances the concluding genealogy and ensures that the dead from the Ephrathite clan, with or without an heir, will not be forgotten. Ironically Elimelech's genealogy at the beginning of the book is one of endings—of death and emptiness. David's genealogy at the end of the book is one of beginnings—of birth and fullness.

Ruth, for whom the book is named, is absent from the concluding genealogy. Why does the writer not include her name in this genealogy so future generations will remember and honor her? After all, Ruth's impassioned loyalty and loving-kindness for her mother-in-law, Naomi, and her courageous commitment to preserving the family name were beyond reproach. All who knew her story recognized her redeeming actions and faithfulness to Israel's LORD. Surely the name of Ruth warrants at least a footnote.

Might Ruth's absence from the genealogy clear her husband and son of Moabite stigma so prevalent during the days of the judges? With Ruth's absence, no Moabite connection appears in the roll call of the generations; David's bloodline emerges pure and intact. Fortunately for Ruth the Gospel according to Matthew serves as a corrective and remembers her as a female ancestor of Jesus. The Gospel of Matthew calls her by name, Ruth the Moabite, and restores to her a rightful place in the Messiah's genealogy—a reminder that foreigners, though excluded by the Israelites, were not overlooked by God. This foreigner had inherited a place in the lineage of Jesus.

Ruth's Moabite ancestry subtly shadows the story from start to finish. The Israelites believed the Moabites to be contemptible, vile, loathsome, and their origin incestuous. The story of the incestuous origin of Moab (Gen. 19:30-38) sheds light on the Israelites' animosity for the Moabites, including Ruth.

The hostility between Moab and Israel began during the Israelites' wanderings in the desert after their escape from Egypt, when the Moabites failed to offer hospitality to the thirsty and hungry wanderers. (For further details read Numbers 22–25.) As time went by, the Hebrew prophets continued to denounce the Moabites for their rudeness, and the Moabites were not allowed to take part in the LORD's assemblies—not even their descendants to the tenth generation. The LORD cautioned the Israelites that for all time they were not to concern themselves with the welfare or prosperity of the Moabites. (Interestingly the Egyptians were not as detestable as the Moabites, since their children of the third generation could be admitted to the assembly of the LORD.) Even after the settlement of Canaan, the enmity continued (Judg. 3:12-30), neither forgotten nor forgiven by either side.

Considering this history of hostility, imagine the deeply held contempt that might have surfaced in the Israelite heart at the reading of Ruth's her-story. The book of Ruth does not mention the ancient enmity between Moabites and Israelites, but the silence about it may speak more loudly than words. Perhaps later generations perceived a broader universal theme in the story—that the LORD's hospitality is decided not by blood and birth or race and nationality, but by faithfulness and commitment to doing the will of God through acts of loving-kindness. No wonder Ruth's loving-kindness and redemptive hospitality undergird the life and ministry of her descendant, Jesus the Messiah.

Ask a Question—Get a Story

If this book is about Ruth, why does the story give so much attention to Naomi as the one in need of redemption? Does the book affirm Ruth as a model of loyalty and faithfulness, or does it subtly and gently erase her presence? Given the Israelite hostility toward the Moabites, how was Elimelech's sojourn into Moab perceived by those he left behind in Bethlehem? Did they consider it an act of disloyalty that may have tainted Naomi's return to Bethlehem, especially when accompanied by Ruth, a Moabite? What risks did Ruth take when she chose to leave her family and country? What kind of bond existed between her and Naomi? What is the nature of the love that moved Ruth to cling to Naomi and vow never to leave her? Was Naomi really the ideal mother-in-law many profess her to be? Given the Hebrew tradition that emphasized the importance of childbearing, was Ruth lifted up and valued primarily for her ability to produce a son? Since the Israelites believed that Moabite women were immoral and corrupt, did the townspeople condemn or tolerate Ruth's unconventional and rather straightforward actions? What did Boaz, a pillar of the community, risk when he married Ruth, a foreigner and a Moabite? What are we to remember about Ruth?

Biblical narrators and editors usually report what was said and done, but not why it was said or how it was done. The reader must fill in the gaps. Like the long-ago biblical audiences who read or listened to Ruth's her-story, we have the wonderful opportunity to note the gaps in the text and to hear what might speak to us in the silences. The rich questions above help us explore details that are mentioned in the text and those that have been excluded. The sacred her-story of Ruth, not exactly a burning bush, still speaks to us of holiness as we approach that which we do not know.

Ruth's persistent loving-kindness and deep love and devotion turned Naomi's life around. Ruth loved Naomi with a fidelity both fierce and gentle. This foreign Moabite, this outsider, extended hospitality and loving-kindness to an Israelite family, her supposed enemy. If we choose to journey with Ruth, we will leave all that is familiar. We will find ourselves in a world of strange social, moral, and religious beliefs. The lives and personalities of the people we meet will mesh with our own. If we choose to enter Ruth's world and live the events of her story from beginning to end, we will glean grain alongside her in the field of Boaz and catch the faint scent of her perfume as she hurries back to Naomi from the threshing floor. If we enter her world and learn from it, perhaps we too might be changed by her loving-kindness.

If we invite Ruth to enter *our* world, we must let Ruth find her way into the caves of our heart's home and into the crannies and crevices of our cluttered minds. She will move into our busy lives and fragile personalities, into our prejudices and intolerance. If we invite Ruth to enter our world, we too might discover that we have been redeemed, that a new self and a new way of loving have been revealed to us. If we choose to speak Ruth's pledge of loyalty to Naomi, we may be invited to lodge with her; her people will be our people and her God our God. Perhaps on this journey we will find anew the God we thought we had left behind.

The First Turning: Remembering

During the time of the judges' rule, Israel had no king; the people did what was right in their own eyes (Judg. 21:25). It was a time of lawlessness and chaos, of violence and insurrection—a hard and perilous time. Instead of rain, blood drenched the soil of the Promised Land. Betrayal, suspicion, and accusations swirled in the air that blew hot, bone-drying the earth. The land refused to blossom. Like the hearts of the people, it was parched, dry, hard as stone—and gave nothing. A famine stalked the land and the breath of the LORD's spirit was quenched, extinguished, dried up.

So Elimelech ("my God is king"), an Ephrathite, left Bethlehem in Judah with his wife, Naomi ("pleasant, pleasure, my sweetness"), and two sons Chilion ("to perish, to pine away") and Mahlon ("sickness, weakling") and went to live in Moab. In the writing of the ancients or in their folktales, characters' names often reflected their destiny or fate. Many scholars suggest the names of the characters in the book of Ruth were intentionally chosen to hint at identity and destiny.

Sojourns into foreign countries to escape famine were common (Gen. 12:10 and 42:1-2). Elimelech's family traveled from Bethlehem to the desert east and around the Dead Sea where they crossed the Jordan River. Opposite the plains of Jericho, they came to the eastern semi-arid steppe of Moab. This area, hard to cultivate and unproductive, provided good grazing land for sheep and goats. Farther east and south on both sides of the Arnon River's deep gorge was the rolling, grain-filled plateau of Moab. This fertile, well-watered strip high above the Dead Sea could produce excellent crops. After traveling many miles from the famine in Bethlehem, through desolate places and across valleys and mountainous cliffs, Elimelech's refugee family must have thought the abundance on the plains of Moab was the Promised Land.

We will never know if the age-old hostility between the Israelites and the Moabites forced Elimelech and his family to live as outsiders in this new land. We do know that Elimelech died and left Naomi a widow with two sons, both of whom lived in Moab about ten years and took Moabite wives. Chilion took Orpah ("the back of the neck," "she who turned away"), and Mahlon took Ruth ("friend, companion, refreshment"). Then tragedy struck again. Chilion and Mahlon both died, leaving Naomi without husband or sons, without any male heirs. This healthy family had earlier departed a sick land only to become sick in a healthy land. Death canceled hope, and Naomi became a stranger in a strange land.

With the deaths of Elimelech and his sons, a subtle nudge from the writer shifts our attention to Naomi. The writer does not refer to Naomi as the widow of Elimelech, the traditional Hebrew expression. Rather Elimelech becomes the "husband of Naomi," and his death does not leave Naomi with Elimelech's sons but with "her two sons." To a modern reader, this insignificant shift may not merit mention. But in Israelite culture a woman generally derived her identity from the name of her husband, son, or other male relative, even if they all were dead. So be alert! While we first thought that Naomi was to be pitied as a powerless widow, the writer has given us a clue that from here on out, Naomi will command the attention. The reader, Orpah, Ruth, Boaz, the women of the town, the elders, the newborn, and even God—all will give their attention to Naomi, the irascible one whose need for redemption turns lives around.

With no heir to support and shelter her, Naomi had no security. Lacking a husband or a son, she could amount to little or nothing. When she heard that the LORD had taken note of the people in Bethlehem and the famine had broken, she decided to return to her homeland. Perhaps the LORD would take note of her extreme circumstances and bestow loving-kindness. Perhaps the Bethlehem townspeople would remember her and take pity on a poor widow. Returning to Bethlehem meant a long and dangerous journey, but Naomi was determined.

Naomi and her two daughters-in-law started on the road that led to the land of Judah, but somewhere along the way Naomi urged each of her daughters-in-law to return to the house of her own mother. Why not instruct them to return to their fathers' houses? Was returning to their mothers' houses the first step in finding security in a husband's house? Perhaps Naomi's instruction meant that Moabite men and women lived in separate quarters. We only know she told her daughters-in-law to leave her, to go back.

Naomi blessed them and wished them future security in the house of a husband. She prayed that the LORD would look upon them with favor and show them the same loving-kindness they had shown to her and her dead family members. The loving-kindness about which Naomi spoke is translated in Hebrew as *chesed.*

Chesed was part of the LORD's very nature, a term used to describe the LORD's relationship to Israel through acts of unexpected and unmerited grace and mercy. *Chesed* shown among members of a family or community meant that loyalty and care had been extended far beyond what the law required. An act of *chesed* entailed the giving of more than could ever be earned or deserved. Naomi's prayer that the LORD's loving-kindness be with Orpah and Ruth as they had been with her implied that the daughters-in-law had gone beyond duty or responsibility. So why did Naomi encourage them to return to Moab?

Naomi kissed her daughters-in-law farewell. They wept aloud, heartbroken that Naomi was turning them away. Still the daughters-in-law persisted in their desire to return with her to her people. Again Naomi urged them to turn back, lamenting that she was too old to have more sons for them to marry. Even if she had married that night and given birth to sons, Naomi believed the situation was hopeless, certain Orpah and Ruth would want to marry before these yet-to-be-conceived sons of her imagination were grown.

Since she had no sons to offer Orpah and Ruth, Naomi felt she had nothing to offer them. As she blessed her daughters-in-law in the LORD's name, Naomi declared that this same LORD's hand had struck out against her and she was worse off than they. Truly Naomi had suffered a great loss, but had she forgotten that her daughters-in-law had experienced the recent deaths of their husbands? that their grief was raw, laid open, and still fresh? that they were young, childless widows? Was Naomi so bitter about her own misfortunes that she failed to comprehend their devotion and love for her? Could she not think beyond her own despair and hopelessness? She believed that the LORD had cursed her and wondered why these young Moabite women wanted to go with her, an older Israelite widow. Again the daughters-in-law wept for Naomi and themselves, for unborn children and unfulfilled dreams.

Naomi's concern that she had no sons for Orpah and Ruth to marry may indicate the practice of the Hebrew levirate law. Since the Hittite, Ugaritic, and Assyrian cultures at that time employed

similar "marriage" customs, it also may have been a Moabite practice. Naomi believed what her Hebrew tradition and religion had
carefully taught her: A woman was of little value without a man.
To live without the protection of a male heir was a terrifying
prospect. Until this situation was remedied, Naomi would remain
bitter and empty, a victim of her culture's attitude toward women.

Up until now, Naomi had recognized Orpah and Ruth as individual women only once. Together she called them her daughters.
Together they went with her. Together they spoke. Together they
wept. Then Orpah made a decision from which she emerged as a
person separate from either Naomi or Ruth: She took the expected
action of a young woman in her situation. She kissed her mother-
in-law and turned to go home. But was that her heart's desire?

Orpah's turning was not a rejection of Naomi or the easier way.
Because her mother-in-law had pleaded with her, Orpah's turning
back became an act of obedience and of loving-kindness (*chesed*),
commitment and respect beyond the requirement. No one condemned Orpah for turning back. Naomi later held up Orpah to
Ruth as the better example. Orpah simply vanished, and, though
remembered, her story remains unfinished. With Orpah's leaving,
Ruth emerges as an individual. Ruth will not vanish from the story,
but will we be invited to experience her fully? Will we find that her
character develops primarily through her devotion to Naomi?

True to her name, Orpah turned back, and as she blended into
the Moabite landscape, all that Ruth and Naomi could see of her
was the back of her neck. But Ruth did not turn back, did not obey
her mother-in-law's bidding. She clung to Naomi and held fast,
refusing to leave. No other recorded incident in the Bible includes
such close physical nearness of one woman to another. Out of
devotion and steadfast loyalty, Ruth clung to her mother-in-law.

From our perspective Ruth did not respond logically. No cultural or legal reasons bound her to Naomi, yet Ruth did the unexplainable as an expression of the same deep loving-kindness that caused Orpah to let go. In a cultural and religious climate where women were of little value without men, Ruth chose to commit her fidelity and love to another woman. Ruth's oath, made in the absence of men and in defiance of the values of the prevailing cultures, testifies to the empowering nature of loving-kindness.

In her years as part of Naomi's family, Ruth had loved her mother-in-law and had learned a little about Naomi's LORD. Perhaps in those hard and troubled years, Naomi's LORD already had become Ruth's refuge; maybe she now wanted to hold fast to this God. Naomi's discounting of Ruth's feelings through her insistence that Ruth abandon her and return to the Moabite people may have frustrated and disheartened Ruth. What could she say to convince Naomi of her heart's true desire? In exasperation and anguish Ruth opened herself to further rejection. Ruth, a Moabite, made a radical decision and solemnly swore her commitment to Naomi in the name of Israel's LORD. If death parted them, Ruth vowed she would leave it to Israel's LORD to deal severely with her if she broke her oath.

After hearing that beautiful expression of loving-kindness, Naomi responded with silence. Expecting some small sign of acknowledgment from her mother-in-law, Ruth must have thought Naomi's heart was deaf. The text does not tell us whether Ruth's words comforted, angered, or awed Naomi. Nor does it indicate that Naomi's silence signaled respect for Ruth's allegiance. Naomi may have feared that Ruth would serve as a constant reminder of her great loss in the land of Moab. Given the history between Moab and Israel, perhaps Naomi anticipated the enmity that might meet her if she showed up with a Moabite daughter-in-law in Bethlehem. If Naomi had already entertained these thoughts and decided to travel alone, Ruth's persistence may have irritated Naomi. Maybe Ruth's clinging was too much, too close, too soon. Whatever the reason for her silence, Naomi carried the emotional baggage of emptiness and bitterness all the way to Bethlehem.

It was probably April, the beginning of the barley harvest, by the time the women made their way into Bethlehem. Their presence stirred the townspeople, and the whole town buzzed with excitement at their arrival. The women of the town asked one another if this truly was Naomi. Perhaps Naomi's return after her long absence surprised them, her appearance and her aged features astonished them. Perhaps they were taken aback by Naomi's Moabite daughter-in-law. Naomi told them she was no longer to be called Naomi ("pleasant, sweet") but Mara ("unpleasant, bitter"). Because the Almighty had filled her life with calamities, her pleasantness had turned to bitterness. She had left full, and through the LORD's doing she returned empty.

Naomi had complained against the LORD to her daughters-in-law on the road from Moab, and she was still complaining when she arrived in Bethlehem. She had left Bethlehem ("the house of bread") all those years ago because of a famine. The breadbasket had been empty. Naomi lamented that she had returned to Bethlehem empty, but she had come back to a fruitful land at a bounteous harvest time. The breadbasket was full. Although Naomi seemed untouched by Ruth's commitment and failed to acknowledge her presence when they arrived in Bethlehem, she did return with a daughter-in-law devoted to her care. She did not return empty as she claimed. By Naomi's side, Ruth silently proved otherwise.

This is Naomi's story, not Ruth's. It is Naomi whose skewed perspective needs righting, whose vision needs correction. It is Naomi whose dark despair needs to be eclipsed by the light of hope. Hers is the life that needs to be turned around, that needs redemption. Again the writer gives us a window through which to glimpse the future. Ruth's faithfulness and loving-kindness will be the catalyst for Naomi's redemption. Naomi may be the subject of God's redemption, but Ruth is the active verb through which that redemption will be accomplished.

For the first time Ruth's her-story refers to her as "Ruth the Moabite" (1:22). While not mentioning the enmity between Moab and Israel, the writer never lets us forget that Ruth is a foreigner, that her Moabite heritage may remain an unforgiven and unforgotten source of contention. The Bethlehem townspeople probably recalled the story about that long-ago incestuous relationship of Lot and his daughters from whom Ruth descended. Despite Ruth's great loving-kindness, they perhaps secretly distrusted this woman of contemptible ancestry. They would never fully accept her into the covenant community, always remaining Ruth the Moabite.

Though safely back in Bethlehem, Ruth and Naomi also were widows who had to feed and care for themselves. By Naomi's earlier admission, she had nothing to offer Ruth for security. But a kinsman of Naomi's dead husband resided in Bethlehem, a man named Boaz ("in him there is strength"). A pillar of the community and a prominent man of substance, Boaz seemingly had no responsibility to assist the women. Did Naomi know or had she forgotten about this kinsman from Elimelech's clan? Surely had she realized the possibility of a close kinsman's providing security for the widows of his dead relatives, she would not have lamented so to her daughters-in-law. With Boaz as a possibility would she have presented herself to the townspeople as a widow who returned empty with only bitterness for her companion?

Ruth had vowed to care and provide for her mother-in-law. Hebrew law provided for those in poverty, including alien strangers, by allowing them to glean in the grainfields after the reapers had passed through. Only the poorest of the poor, native or alien, would demean themselves by gleaning. That Ruth offered to do so indicates the destitution in which she and Naomi now found themselves. Ruth hoped she might find favor and an offer of kindness as she gleaned. When Ruth told her mother-in-law of her intent to glean, the silence between them was broken. "Go, my daughter," Naomi said. No expression of gratitude, no blessing or farewell. Just go. Nothing more, nothing less. Perhaps when Ruth heard these words, she recalled another time not too distant when Naomi had told her to go.

A grainfield was not the safest place for young women. Without protection, they were sometimes harassed or assaulted by the reapers. Additionally, gleaning was hard work. Naomi had not cautioned Ruth about what she might expect. A young Moabite woman alone in unpredictable circumstances, Ruth must have been anxious and fearful. Being an outsider and a childless widow made her quite vulnerable. Ruth probably suspected she could be considered an easy conquest for the men. But Naomi and Ruth needed food, so she went to the barley fields to glean.

As chance would have it, Ruth found herself in the section of the field that belonged to Boaz just as he arrived from Bethlehem. Boaz greeted the reapers with a formal salutation of respect that older citizens frequently used: "The LORD be with you." The reapers responded with a blessing: "The LORD bless you!" This brief exchange suggests Boaz was a godly man with a kind spirit who cared for his workers.

Ruth must have been nearby or else she stood out among the others because Boaz immediately noticed her. He asked his supervisor to whom the young woman belonged. In those days every woman belonged to a man—a husband, a son, a brother, or a master. Boaz might even have been inquiring about her lineage. Apparently not knowing to whom Ruth belonged, the supervisor confided that she was the Moabite girl who had accompanied Naomi from the plains of Moab. Did his knowledge of this information mean that everyone in the village knew Naomi and her business?

Ruth's persistence must have impressed the supervisor. He told Boaz that she had been on her feet early and all day with no rest. As a Moabite, Ruth may have waited all day to get special permission from the landowner to glean. While the law permitted the poor to glean grain missed by the reapers *after* the sheaves of grain were bundled and removed from the field and to gather grain along the edges and corners of the field, the actual opportunity to glean and gather depended on the landowner's goodwill. Ruth's request to glean and gather among the sheaves *before* they had been carried off the field was a departure from the Hebrew law. Perhaps Ruth's request was one of pure innocence (or could it have been bold determination?). If Ruth went to the field with the intention of finding favor in someone's eyes, her plan worked. Boaz was about to offer generosity that went beyond his duty or responsibility. Ruth wanted and needed the favor of kindness (*chesed*), and through Boaz she would receive it.

Boaz spoke to Ruth, calling her daughter. This greeting may have been the traditional one of an older man to a younger woman. It may have designated status, a clear indication that Boaz was Ruth's superior. Although unlikely that Ruth knew this was Naomi's kinsman, his greeting may have served to acknowledge a family connection between them. With no further conversation, Boaz heaped one exceptional favor of *chesed* after another on Ruth: She should glean in no field but his during the harvest season, keeping close to his young women; his young men would not touch or bother her. She should drink from water drawn by his men when thirsty and eat the roasted grain with his reapers when hungry. She should glean among the bundled sheaves still standing in the field. The reapers would not scold or humiliate her; they would pull out handfuls of grain stalks and leave them for her to glean. This special treatment certainly would have been perceived as loving-kindness (*chesed*) beyond any obligation or duty.

Ruth first responded to Boaz's unexpected kindness and hospitality by bowing with her face to the ground and asking why he had noticed her, a foreigner. Foreigners, especially foreign widows, usually did not receive favorable recognition or treatment. The townspeople, including Boaz, may have observed Ruth's untiring devotion to Naomi. Perhaps they had noticed that even at Naomi's worst, Ruth still loved and cared for her. Boaz had heard about the good works Ruth had done for her mother-in-law, leaving her family and homeland to come to a people she did not know.

In Hebrew tradition a man left his father and mother, traveled to a foreign land, endured hardship, and lived among people he did not know (Gen. 29; Exod. 2:15-22). Abraham left his country because of God's call that promised great blessings; he took his wife and possessions with him. Abraham stood within the Hebrew tradition. Ruth left her country with no possessions, no family (except her mother-in-law), no call from God, and no promise of any blessings. Contrary to Naomi, who believed that a woman's value lay in bearing children, Boaz recognized that Ruth's loving-kindness made her a worthy woman in her own right, and he wished for Ruth a full reward from the LORD, the God of Israel, under whose wings she had come for refuge.

Believing that Boaz, this man of substance, might be a person who could assist her mother-in-law, Ruth asserted herself. Ruth might have wondered if Boaz's words hinted at more than they said. Perhaps he found her attractive. Maybe his concern for her well-being had an ulterior motive. Yet she addressed Boaz respectfully as "my lord" and said she hoped always to find favor in his sight. She told him that his kind and gentle words comforted her, his "servant" (even though she was not one of his servants).

Behind her words, perhaps Ruth was sending an unspoken message to Boaz. Did Ruth mean that his words had encouraged her, or had they spoken tenderly to her heart? To speak kindly or tenderly to the heart implied an intimate expression sometimes used in courtship with the subtle intention to woo, persuade, or convince. (See Gen. 34:3; Judg. 19:3; Hos. 2:14.) Perhaps Ruth intended to speak tenderly to Boaz's heart even as he had spoken tenderly to hers. She had reminded him that she was his servant—but not really. Maybe Ruth meant to suggest that Boaz's kindness and favors obligated him to care for her. She may have aimed to clear the way for a relationship between them if Boaz so chose.

Ruth did not return to Naomi empty-handed. After Naomi saw how much barley Ruth had brought home to her, she knew that Ruth had benefited from someone's generosity. When Ruth gave her the roasted grain left from the meal that Boaz had served her, Naomi knew an unusual event had taken place. Without a word of thanks but forthrightly and insistently Naomi asked Ruth where she had gleaned that day, blessing the man who had taken such favorable notice of Ruth. Ruth told Naomi where she had gleaned and that the name of the man who owned the field was Boaz. Naomi called the Lord's name as she again blessed the man for their good fortune, but Ruth attributed their good fortune to Boaz.

As Ruth relayed the day's events, Naomi's despondency gave way to an awakened hope at Ruth's good news. Now Naomi knew that neither the living nor the dead were forsaken. Naomi finally included Ruth in her family circle, referring to Boaz as a relative of "ours" and one of "our" nearest kin. But why did Naomi only then recall Boaz, one of their *nearest* relatives? Maybe Ruth's Moabite roots made Naomi reluctant to ask Boaz for assistance. Perhaps she thought he had an obligation to seek out his dead relatives' widows. Maybe she was even waiting for the tradition of the levirate bond to work the way it used to. Taking note of Boaz's obvious interest in Ruth, Naomi may have seen the possibility of a relationship that would solve the problems of Ruth and herself.

Ruth, desiring Naomi's further affirmation and approval or wanting to show her mother-in-law she could make a way for them, disclosed to Naomi that Boaz had invited her to glean with the reapers in his field. Expressing concern that harm might come to Ruth if she changed fields, Naomi encouraged Ruth to glean only in Boaz's field. Naomi's concern sounded genuine and very motherly—or did it? Behind her caution may have been a more selfish motivation. With the possibility of a relationship between Ruth and Boaz that would benefit her, Naomi may have feared Ruth's attraction to one of the younger workers. But Ruth followed Naomi's instructions to glean with the young women during the harvest season, which lasted about seven weeks. Then Ruth stayed home with Naomi and cared for her. They lived on the barley and wheat that Ruth had gleaned. After Boaz's initial interest in Ruth, apparently nothing happened between them. And nothing changed for Ruth and Naomi, widows with no means of support except begging or gleaning. With the gleaning season now over, they had to find some further means of support.

The two widows Ruth and Naomi were probably vulnerable to exploitation, but did the severity of their situation necessitate what happened next? Though the sexually suggestive double meanings in Ruth's her-story may offend our modern sensibilities, an ancient Hebrew audience would have understood and delighted in them.

Naomi wanted to see Ruth settled with some security, which meant finding a husband. Naomi put together a plan she hoped would provide some security for them both, but its success would depend on Ruth. Knowing Boaz would be at the threshing floor that night, Naomi had Ruth prepare herself as a bride in the

Hebrew tradition. Ruth bathed, anointed, and perfumed herself, dressed in the finest clothes, and went to the place where the "bridegroom" was waiting. She was not to make herself known to Boaz until he had finished eating and drinking. After Boaz had settled down for the night, Ruth was to go to him, uncover his feet, and lie down beside him. Naomi assured Ruth that Boaz would tell her what to do next! Ruth pledged to carry out Naomi's instructions.

The grain could not be bagged or transported until after the winnowing process, so the landowner spent the night near the threshing floor. Naomi must have known this. She also knew that the activity surrounding the winnowing and threshing of the grain was a raucous and wild affair, long associated with drinking and loose women (Hos. 9:1). The Bethlehem prostitutes would provide the evening's main entertainment. The threshing floor was not the place for a virtuous woman. Yet Naomi sent her daughter-in-law, a young widow from Moab, to the threshing floor. What was Naomi thinking? Did Ruth do as she was told to please her mother-in-law? Or did she have plans of her own to get from Boaz what she wanted and needed? Throughout the Hebrew Bible the terms *to know* and *to lie with* are euphemisms for sexual intimacy. The term *uncover* often refers to sexual intercourse (Lev. 18:6-19). The root word in Hebrew for feet means lower body, which includes the genitals. We rightly wonder about Naomi and Ruth's motivations.

About midnight something startled the sleeping Boaz. He woke up and was shocked to find a young woman lying at his uncovered feet. One ancient rabbi wrote, "When Boaz saw a woman at his feet, his flesh became weak as a turnip."

Boaz asked Ruth who she was. He no longer had an interest in knowing to whom she belonged; rather, he wanted to know Ruth's personal identity. In that moment and on her own, Ruth upgraded her status from foreigner to servant, communicating to Boaz her availability for a relationship, with marriage as a possibility. Perhaps

Boaz feared that he, like Ruth's ancestor Lot, had awakened in a stupor with no memory of what he had done. Perhaps he wondered if they had already engaged in sexual activity.

Ruth had followed Naomi's instructions, and now was no time for shyness. Instead of waiting for Boaz to tell her what to do, in a bold move she told him what to do. Ruth made an unconventional request of Boaz: that he spread the edge or wings of his cloak over her. The Hebrew words for cloak and wing come from the common root word *kanaph*. Their meaning is the same: "to spread over." Earlier in the story Boaz had wished for Ruth a full reward from God, under whose wings she had come for refuge. Now on the threshing floor Ruth requested refuge under the wings of Boaz's cloak, appealing to Boaz not as a relative of her dead husband but as her redeemer.

Chapter 3 of Ruth may clarify Ruth's understanding of Boaz's right of redemption over her. This chapter in the New Revised Standard Version of the Bible uses the term *next-of-kin* seven times. Other translations use *redeemer* and *redeeming kinsman*—all with the same connotation. A redeemer was a family member who had the right of redemption, the obligation and duty to provide security, especially for widows and the poor; to restore the honor and prestige of the family; and to protect the interests, property, and inheritance of his extended family. A redeemer's responsibility did not include marrying the widow of a dead relative and providing an heir unless he was the *levir* (brother).

Ruth's request both surprised and pleased Boaz. His gracious response was but another indication of his kindness. Boaz asked the LORD to bless Ruth, but she already had encouraged him once in the field to make those blessings come true for her himself. Now for a second time she intimated that Boaz could do for her what seemed to be taking the LORD too long to do. Perhaps Ruth offered Boaz a way to pursue his inclination. By proposing that

Boaz claim his right of redemption over her, she gave him a socially acceptable reason for their relationship. Boaz might have begun to understand that he could separate Ruth's request for protection and shelter from his duty to provide security and protection for Naomi, a solution that extended his loving-kindness far beyond his responsibility to fulfill the law. This solution would secure not only the futures of Naomi and Ruth but also his.

Boaz recognized that Ruth, unbound by the levirate law and free to marry anyone she chose, had not turned to younger men, rich or poor, but to him. He praised Ruth for her loyalty and loving-kindness and for her commitment to protect her mother-in-law and secure a redeemer for her, perceiving that Ruth's first commitment was to family loyalty and solidarity and to the continuity of Naomi's family. Boaz assured Ruth that he and all the townspeople knew she was a worthy woman and that he would do all she asked. (But for what exactly had she asked?) Perhaps Boaz meant she was no longer his servant, but that she was fit to be his wife. *Servant*, often a term of politeness, did not necessarily define a role in a relationship. Boaz's assurance that he would do all Ruth asked was his pledge and covenant to Ruth that he would spread the edges of his cloak over her and give her refuge. In other words, Boaz agreed to be her redeeming kinsman and marry her.

Ruth was not alone in the ability to use an unguarded moment for surprise. After Boaz had agreed to do all she had asked, he made an unexpected announcement to Ruth, disclosing that there was a kinsman more closely related than he who had the first right of redemption. Boaz obviously knew about this closer redeemer before the threshing floor meeting, so why did he wait to tell Ruth? He may have been waiting throughout the harvest season for this kinsman to come forward and claim his right of redemption, but Ruth's request for redemption had forced the issue. Now he could no longer ignore it. He would have to find a way to resolve it. Marrying Ruth was one thing; securing Naomi's inheritance was another matter—one that would require negotiation with the nearest kinsman. To Boaz's credit he confessed to Ruth the existence of the closer redeemer and did not attempt to bypass the directive of the Hebrew inheritance laws.

It probably was quite late when Boaz suggested that Ruth stay the rest of the night with him. By this time the walk by herself back into Bethlehem might have been unsafe. Boaz comforted her with the promise that he would speak with the other redeemer come morning. Even if that redeemer chose not to claim his right of redemption, Boaz renewed his pledge to Ruth, swearing in the name of the Lord that he would. So Ruth lay down at Boaz's feet until early morning. Before it was light enough for anyone to be recognized, Boaz discreetly sent Ruth away, enjoining her not to reveal that she had come to the threshing floor.

Even innocent conversation between Ruth and Boaz during the night would have been too much for the townspeople. That a Moabite woman had uncovered an Israelite man's feet and slept next to a man not her husband would have been more than scandalous. The mere fact of Ruth's presence on the threshing floor with Boaz would have been considered promiscuous behavior, damaging permanently her reputation as a worthy and virtuous woman. Boaz's reputation as a pillar of the community also would have suffered. For Boaz's plan of redemption to work, the nearest redeemer must know nothing about this night. Otherwise his motive in negotiating with the closer redeemer might be perceived as sexual desire rather than responsible business dealing, which would jeopardize Boaz's redemptive intentions.

Boaz did not send Ruth away empty-handed but filled the cloak she wore with six measures of barley. Was this just a thoughtful ges-

ture to a widow and her Moabite daughter-in-law? Or was the grain
a gift to appease Naomi for Ruth's absence during the night? Perhaps it was a bride-price or a marriage settlement or merely a pledge
to let Naomi know that Boaz intended to claim his right of
redemption over Ruth. Regardless of Boaz's intent, Naomi knew
that this gift sent a message to her, and she did not hesitate to ask
Ruth the question that had been on her mind all through the night.
She inquired how things had gone with Ruth. The Hebrew translation of this phrase literally means, "Who are you?" Perhaps
Naomi had failed to recognize Ruth in the lingering darkness. In
fact Boaz had asked Ruth the same question the night before when
he had failed to recognize her on the threshing floor. Naomi likely
was curious to know if her plan had worked; Ruth's response must
have pleased her.

Ruth told Naomi all that Boaz had done for her but did not
tell all that *she* had done. She did not mention her initiative in having Boaz spread the edge of his cloak over her and becoming her
redeemer. Nor did she tell Naomi of a marriage proposal or of
another redeemer who was closer than Boaz. But Ruth did credit
Boaz for saying something he had not said, that she should not go
back to her mother-in-law empty-handed, which resulted in the six
measures of barley. At Ruth's report, Naomi's emptiness and
despair changed to happiness, her bitterness to sweetness.

Ruth's last spoken message from the book of Ruth expressed
commitment and concern for Naomi's security and well-being.
From this time forth, Ruth will become the passive and traditional
childbearing wife of Boaz; she will remain without voice. Naomi
astutely and shrewdly offered her last tidbit of advice to Ruth:
"Wait, my daughter, until you learn how the matter turns out,"
which indicated Naomi's certainty that Boaz would not rest until
the situation was resolved. Meanwhile Boaz had gone to the city
gate. Just inside the gate was a courtyard area with benches where

people gathered to discuss town business, to settle disputes between citizens, to validate contracts, and even to mete out punishment. With elders of the town and other citizens serving as witnesses or as a jury, a court of law convened.

The meeting between Boaz and his relative at the gate of the city probably was not coincidental. Probably knowing when his relative would pass that way, Boaz "just happened to be there." Boaz invited the man to sit down and then gathered ten elders of the town. Making his case before the elders, Boaz explained that Naomi had returned from the country of Moab and must sell the parcel of her dead husband's land, which the nearest kinsman should buy in the presence of the elders and others seated there. If the kinsman so chose, he should claim his right of redemption in that moment. If not, he should tell Boaz, since no one else had the right of redemption as long the closest redeemer had not made a claim. Boaz also noted that the right of redemption passed to him after this kinsman. (Interestingly, for the first time the writer makes clear in this scene that Elimelech's land had passed on to Naomi—not to Ruth. This information separates the issue of Naomi's property and inheritance from the issue of Ruth's freedom to marry.) The kinsman agreed to redeem Naomi's land and probably thought, along with the elders and witnesses, that the deal was completed. But Boaz was not finished with his proposition.

Showing a shadow side of himself that may have been more self-serving than virtuous, Boaz, the man of unanticipated revelations, continued to outline the conditions for redemption rights according to his plan, which differed from tradition. In an unexpected and unprecedented legal declaration, Boaz disclosed that with the acquisition of Naomi's property, the kinsman would also acquire Ruth the Moabite. Now this bit of information came as a surprise. The kinsman was probably even more stunned to learn that in acquiring the Moabite widow, he was obligated to protect and provide security for her, so that the property might revert to Elimelech's family if Ruth bore an heir. Ruth is identified throughout this entire section only as the dead man's widow or the dead man's wife. She is never referred to as Ruth or even as Naomi's daughter-in-law. (Is Ruth gradually beginning to fade from sight?)

Perhaps we should examine more closely this business transaction at the city gate between Boaz and the nearest kinsman. The real issue was the redemption of the land to prevent it from being separated from Elimelech's family. Redeeming the land in order to maintain the dead man's name (Mahlon, Ruth's dead husband) simply meant that if Ruth had a son, he could legally claim the land that had been recovered by the redeemer. With an inheritance claim on it, the land would revert to Mahlon's heir.

The acquisition of Ruth might have implied marrying her and producing a son to perpetuate the dead man's name on Elimelech's property. But land redemption did not depend on a levirate marriage. If this had been the case, Naomi would not have urged Ruth to return to her mother's house in Moab, since she knew that a levirate marriage was the only way of rescuing the inheritance of a man who had died childless. Yet Boaz made a strategic move when he presented acquisition of the land and acquisition of Ruth as a package deal to the kinsman, who then assumed these two things belonged together. It was to Boaz's advantage to have the nearest kinsman understand the deal this way.

The kinsman-redeemer probably had a vested interest in the right of redemption as long as it would benefit him, his heirs, and his estate. He knew that both Naomi and Ruth were widows with no heirs. If he decided to redeem the property, he reasoned, these two widows would not threaten his claim on the land as part of his estate. But Boaz claimed that with Ruth as part of the acquisition the redeemer was duty-bound to ensure the perpetuation of the dead man's name on the property. The kinsman-redeemer had to reconsider, since he was not willing to take responsibility for the security of the women through whom he would receive the land and its benefits. Had this been a true levirate marriage situation, the kinsman's refusal would have been a serious breach of the levirate law, but there was no censure of him by the elders of the city for his decision not to act as redeemer.

We now enter the part of Ruth's her-story where complexities seemingly never resolve themselves. Scholars and commentators have confessed that this section makes them anxious because they have been unsuccessful in unraveling it to their satisfaction. So we are in good company!

By negotiating his business at the city gate openly and by manipulating the kinsman-redeemer into believing the inseparable nature of land acquisition and Ruth, Boaz succeeded in getting the kinsman-redeemer to withdraw any claim to Elimelech's property or to Ruth. With his knowledge of the complexities of the law, Boaz masterfully worked the system to get what he wanted without estranging the elders or the townspeople from Ruth or himself. But Boaz risked losing the land and Ruth if events did not go as he projected.

That the writer has to explain what happened next—the ritual of "unsandaling"—alerts us to the probability that Ruth's her-story was presented to an audience unfamiliar with the custom. This fact may indicate that the book of Ruth was written at a later time when this ritual was seldom or no longer practiced. In former times in Israel (during the time of Ruth and Boaz) sandals signaled the prosperity of the wearer. Slaves, servants, and poor people went barefoot, so the exchange of a sandal occurred only among men of substance and stability. Throwing a sandal on disputed land was one way of claiming property ownership. The procedure described in Ruth does not strictly adhere to Hebrew law (Deut. 25:5-10). Over time and in different geographical regions, the ritual may have been altered to accommodate local customs and conditions.

The ritual for the redemption or exchange of land in Ruth's her-story went like this: One man took off his sandal or shoe and handed it to the other as a sign that a legal transaction had been ratified. When the kinsman took off his sandal and handed it to Boaz, he transferred his right of redemption to Boaz and gave up any legal claim to the land belonging to Elimelech. Rather than rejecting a levirate marriage, the nearest kinsman declined a business proposal without being discredited or repudiated.

Again Boaz made clear his intentions before the elders and the people assembled, calling them witnesses to his first public declaration: that he had acquired from Naomi all that had belonged to Elimelech, Chilion, and Mahlon. Only then did Boaz declare that he also had acquired Ruth the Moabite, the widow of Mahlon, to be his wife. The term *acquire* has at least two possible meanings in the context of this story: (1) Boaz had bought both the property and Ruth. (In a levirate marriage situation, the levirate widow is not bought. She is already considered to be under the authority of the levir.) (2) Boaz had made both the property and Ruth legally his own, thus freeing him to take Ruth as his wife. The elders and witnesses did not know that Boaz already had made Ruth his own when he covered her with the edge of his cloak and pledged that she would have refuge under his wing. The latter interpretation, to make what is acquired one's own, seems more in keeping with the other events of the story.

Having acquired Ruth as his wife, Boaz pledged to keep the dead man's name on the inheritance of land so that his name would not disappear from the memory of his kindred or be missing from the gate of his hometown of Bethlehem. Naomi would become a protected widow whose property had been redeemed and whose needs would be secured. Boaz claimed his covenant responsibility for Naomi's family, not because the law demanded it but because loving-kindness (*chesed*) demanded it. He did not hope to receive the Lord's loving favor but to live out the Lord's loving-kindness on behalf of others. Boaz sealed this legal transaction by again proclaiming to the elders and the gathered people that they served as his witnesses.

The community sanctioned Boaz's announcement that Ruth would be his wife and pronounced a collective blessing in the name of the Lord. Usually a man was recognized and blessed first. But this community performed the unusual act of recognizing and blessing first the Moabite woman who was to be Boaz's wife! They wished for Ruth, a Moabite, fertility like that of Rachel and Leah, the two Israelite women who built up the house of Israel. The community's blessing affirmed their cultural values—that Ruth's worth lay in bearing many sons. For Boaz the community wished prosperity with moral strength and temporal power, a name famous and perpetuated in Bethlehem, and offspring to rival the house of Perez, whom Tamar bore to Judah. Fertility and fruitfulness—these were the blessings of the community on Ruth and Boaz.

The community's blessings on Ruth were cast in the shadowed silhouettes of strong assertive women. Rachel was the matriarch of the northern kingdom's dominant tribe and the mother of Joseph, the half brother of Judah. Leah was the matriarch of the southern kingdom's dominant tribe and mother of Judah, the father of Perez. Rachel and Leah, two sisters, were the wives (at the same time) of Jacob, the patriarch of Israel, whose house they built up into the Twelve Tribes.

Ephrath was the mother of the clan of Ephrathites from whom Elimelech, Chilion, and Mahlon were descended. Tamar was a

Canaanite and the mother of Perez through an uncustomary act with her father-in-law, Judah. Ruth the Moabite was a descendant of an incestuous relationship between Lot and his older daughter. Since Lot was Father Abraham's nephew, Ruth's lineage had roots buried deep in the beginnings of the LORD's covenant people. It takes a woman to perpetuate a man's name, whether he is dead or alive! The ancient sages believed the LORD enabled, allowed, made, and caused all the female ancestors, including Ruth, to conceive and bear sons. There were no accidents or mistakes in this lineage.

Boaz may have acquired Ruth through a legal transaction and the toss of a sandal, but as Israelite men had done for centuries before him, Boaz "took" Ruth and made her his wife. When Boaz and Ruth came together in sexual union the LORD's loving-kindness was womb-close. In a divine activity thought possible only by the LORD's will, Ruth conceived and bore a son. Here Ruth's participation in the story ends: "And she bore a son." Ruth had pledged her life and her death to Naomi on the road from Moab to Bethlehem and had provided care and sustenance for her. Ruth's devotion (loving-kindness) to Naomi went far beyond any duty or obligation. In a last gesture of devotion, she fulfilled her mother-in-law's deepest hunger by giving Naomi an heir.

Ruth now departs from the story, and Boaz apparently has served his purpose. Loving-kindness has not just recovered Naomi's parcel of land; it has recovered her name and her sense of identity as well. The birth of Ruth's son by Boaz will maintain the property of Elimelech and Mahlon for perpetuity. But Ruth's son will perpetuate the name of Boaz—not Mahlon—down through the ages. Boaz's loving-kindness has done its work. Yet because this is Naomi's story (remember?), a man, even one as substantial as Boaz, is no longer necessary. Naomi and the boy child are the only characters of the story who remain. Well, not quite. The women of the town still have some unfinished business.

The women who first welcomed Naomi back to Bethlehem had suffered Naomi's bitterness throughout the harvest season. They knew all along that Naomi needed to be redeemed—to have her life changed—and that such redemption went beyond property lines, perimeters of inheritance, and obligations of protection. When Ruth bore a son, these women blessed the LORD, for Naomi would not be left alone. They reminded Naomi that the LORD, turned against her no longer, had given this boy child to be her nearest kinsman-redeemer, and they prayed that his name might become famous in Israel, for he would restore Naomi's life.

While the townswomen upheld and blessed Ruth as the bearer of the child rather than Boaz as the begetter, they recognized that Ruth's true value resided in the measure of her love. Her loving-kindness was what counted, not just her fertility. The women told Naomi that Ruth had been better to her than seven sons. Seven, a special number in the Jewish tradition, symbolized completeness. To have seven sons was the ultimate of family blessings. In a patriarchal culture where the number of sons determined the mother's status and economic security, the claim that one daughter-in-law was worth more than seven sons called into question the basic premise and structure of Israelite society. Yet the women of Bethlehem made the claim anyway.

Naomi took the child of Ruth and Boaz and held him to her bosom and cared for him. In regions of the ancient Near East close to where the Israelites lived, a symbolic adoption ritual designated a special relationship to a child, perhaps similar to the role of a godparent. Through just such a relationship, what seemed impossible at the beginning of the story had come true. Naomi had a son!—a kinsman-redeemer who was the heir of Elimelech and Mahlon as well. Not Boaz but the women of the town named the child. They called him Obed ("servant of the LORD," "worker for God"). He became the father of Jesse, father of David. Though the townswomen spoke their final words of praise to Naomi, Ruth the Moabite was remembered by later generations as the ancestral mother of Jesus, heir to David's earthly messiahship.

The quiet revolution of townswomen brought about a subtle reversal of the way things had always been done: a better way that honored the women of the family, mothers and grandmothers along with the fathers and grandfathers; that honored birth and life, not just the names of dead men; that honored selfless love more than inheritance. In quiet, unobtrusive ways, the women of Bethlehem claimed their rights of redemption to change patriarchal traditions where they could. In small transformations here and there, they safeguarded Ruth's her-story as a woman's story. Whether Ruth's story or Naomi's, a strong voice is the chorus of women in the background from the time Naomi and Ruth arrived in Bethlehem until the end. It is they who have the final word—Obed.

Obed, the "root" of David's family tree, was the son of a Moabite foreigner Ruth, who had an unusual meeting on a threshing floor with a man of Israel named Boaz. His grandmother, Rahab, a Canaanite prostitute, "entertained" two Israelite spies in Jericho. Another female ancestor, Tamar, was a Canaanite who boldly sought to gain from her father-in-law, Judah, through unconventional and unorthodox actions what was rightfully hers. For the purists among the Israelite aristocracy and religious authorities who insisted on keeping bloodlines pure as a sign of holiness and obedience to the LORD, the inclusion of Ruth, Rahab, and Tamar in the official genealogy must have seemed almost too scandalous to bear. But in changing times and unpredictable circumstances these women moved out in faith and sought to do what was right and just. Their faith, not their nationality or bloodline, commended them as mothers of kings and the Messiah.

The genealogy may have been traced through the fathers, but the mother roots of these women—embedded in her-story—have nurtured and sustained the messianic line throughout the centuries. The women kept family circles from being broken and redeemed family names, and some, contrary to Israelite customs and traditions, refused to be submissive and docile. The names and her-stories of Tamar, Rahab, and Ruth are recorded in the genealogy of Jesus the Messiah as declarations that bold and assertive women find favor with God.

Her-Story Embedded in History

The story of Ruth may seem idyllic, bathed as it is in loving-kindness and absent of violence or rancor. Yet when read more closely, it yields suffering, death, despair, and fear of abandonment. We may feel that we are finished with this story, but Ruth's her-story is not finished with us. It invites us to return to a possibility that we have given only a passing nod, and one that will further our discernment about the important connections between Ruth and the history of the Israelites. With Ruth ("beloved, friend, companion") we find ourselves at the crossroads of both patriarchal and monarchical history. Standing at the center of the crossroads, Ruth bids us investigate more closely the ties that bind these two histories together.

Looking backward to the stories of Abraham with Lot and his two daughters, Judah with Tamar, Elimelech with Naomi, and Ruth with Boaz, we may better see the connections among Obed, King David, and Jesus of Nazareth ("the Son of David"). All of these stories begin with separation in a foreign land, followed by tragedy and misfortune. After Lot and Abraham left each other, Lot experienced destruction and death in his new home of Sodom and Gomorrah (Gen. 13:1-13; 19:12-26). After Judah left his brothers and father, his two sons and wife died (Gen. 38:1-12).

Elimelech departed Bethlehem during a famine and traveled to Moab where he and his two sons died (Ruth 1:1-5). Ruth's experience illustrated that a woman as well as a man may choose to leave her family and journey to a foreign land. Though a destitute and maligned outsider, she found her burden lightened by the LORD's loving-kindness.

Lot's daughters, Tamar and Ruth were childless. They realized the possible jeopardy of a particular Israelite lineage even though the men did not. The secret and sometimes deceptive initiatives of these women perpetuated the family. Death gave way to life, emptiness to fullness, despair to hope, and a lineage that might have ended was restored.

In spite of the social evolution and moral development in these family chronicles, age-old separations kept families and tribes apart, and past animosities fueled unforgiven hatred. This history needed to be redeemed and the families reunited. Ruth seemed an improbable person to begin healing the family tree, but through her, redemption and reunion were effected. Having come from the branch of Moab, when grafted into the tree of Abraham through Boaz, she bore the fruit of Obed, who would help fulfill the patriarchal promise and covenant (Gen. 12:1-3).

The writer of the book of Ruth established the continuity of the covenant history that began with the patriarchs, especially Abraham, and ended with King David and his royal house. Just as this continuity bound together Judah and Tamar with the patriarchal covenant and promise, it also linked them to Ruth and Boaz, who were bound together with the royal fulfillment of the Davidic dynasty. With Ruth came the possible healing in the family tree of faithful Abraham and his recalcitrant nephew Lot. Her marriage to Boaz narrowed the chasm between Judah and Moab. Reconciliation became a possibility. The reuniting of these patriarchal ties opened a new path of salvation and blessing to all earth's families.

Ruth's her-story strongly emphasizes the continuity between God's promise to Abraham and to the Davidic monarchy, while excluding any reference to Moses or the patriarchal figures of the Mosaic era. Israel's historical and theological past in relation to the Exodus and the Sinaitic covenant is absent. With no apparent regard for these watershed experiences that led to the formidable and inflexible holiness laws and codes, the book of Ruth links together the other patriarchal covenant in Israel's history: Through Abraham all peoples of the earth will be blessed. While Ruth bridged this gap for the Israelites, she also bridged it for Christians. The history and theology of the Abrahamic covenant nourished the roots and prepared the fertile soil that brought forth Jesus the Messiah, who came as the "Son of David" to fulfill the promises and prophecies of the patriarchs, to be God's loving-kindness incarnate.

The same Bethlehem ("house of bread") to which Ruth came as a foreigner would bring forth the true Bread of Life. The same Bethlehem fields in which Ruth gleaned and gathered would hear the sounds of heavenly hosts proclaiming peace and goodwill to all families of the earth. In Jesus the manifestation of Abraham's covenant born in human flesh persevered in binding up and healing the wounds of a fractured world. Jesus, the beloved, friend, and companion continued the reconciliation of all creation foreseen by Ruth, who had brought about the binding together of Abraham's family tree.

The Second Turning: Reading between the Lines

The book of Ruth does not lack themes, among them the following: coming to know oneself through involvement with others, finding acceptance and fulfillment of our inner selves in relationship with others, and extending loving-kindness that goes beyond duty or responsibility.

Loving-kindness is a theme that characterizes the relationships throughout the story. The writer of the book of Ruth makes it clear that Ruth, Boaz, and Naomi were not always prompted by pure motives. Yet within their complex and layered relationships each engaged in redemptive acts of loving-kindness. Doing the right thing does not require perfection or absolute righteousness; it requires a contrite heart of loving-kindness. The LORD bestows loving-kindness on us not because we merit it but because loving-kindness is the LORD's very nature. As recipients of the LORD's gracious plenty, we are deemed worthy and called to be advocates of that same loving-kindness in all our human relationships.

Loving-kindness is redemption's companion. Naomi, Ruth, and Boaz experienced redemption not because they earned it or deserved it but as gift of the LORD's loving-kindness. Our good works and faithfulness do not guarantee our redemption. We are redeemed because the LORD's faithfulness clings to us, keeps close to us, and will not let us go. And when redeeming kindness finds us out and uncovers us, we discover that our essential nature has been recovered and restored.

Ruth the Moabite, the embodiment of love and loyalty, kindles a corresponding response of love and loyalty in Boaz and Naomi. Ruth reminds us that the LORD takes pleasure in those who do not fit religious or social expectations and standards. The LORD's wings spread wide enough to shelter the outcast and foreigner, the flawed and disreputable, the hopeless and desperate, the misfits and rejects. The LORD often chooses those who live on the boundary to accomplish redemptive purposes in the world.

As a messenger of redemption, Ruth reveals much about the Giver of the message. The Israelite's LORD Almighty and our God lived on the boundary and wandered to unfamiliar places. Where there was no family, this God created a family. Where there was a people in an unknown land, this God tented among them. This

God continues to wander and tent, to live at the edge and in-between and beyond, to search out the "other" to redeem. This God's loving-kindness never runs out—not for them, not for us.

Women's Rights Are Human Rights

We do not know how the people of Bethlehem treated Ruth the Moabite upon her arrival. When strictly enforced, Hebrew law would exclude her from the Israelites' assembly of the LORD. A foreigner arriving in a strange country and settling among a people who believed their Lord favored them above all others, Ruth probably had limited access to Hebrew religious festivals and services. A childless and poor widow, she might have found the doors to Bethlehem society closed to her. Had the law been practiced as prescribed when Ruth came into the city, parts of Ruth's her-story would read quite differently. Yet in the end, she was upheld as a model of loving-kindness and blessed by the townspeople.

We live in a world culture of exclusion. All of us in one way or another practice the sin of exclusion, and most of us have felt its sting. We choose not to accept some into our hearts, homes, schools, and churches. Governments, corporations, organizations, and groups of all kinds exclude. Ethnic, racial, economic, educational, religious, cultural, and social differences, big or little, all become reasons to exclude. Wars are fought, discrimination practiced, and humiliation justified in the name of exclusion.

Choosing to exclude constitutes a form of oppressive violence, which is obsessed with and driven by the power to control what we do not understand. Exclusion propelled by fear can breed unrestrained and savage violence with the potential to mushroom into barbaric and brutal explosions, showering fallout in all corners of the world. No one escapes the effects of exclusion that generates fear and violence and shatters promise and hope.

One form of exclusion has developed with the impact of rapid globalization, which has dramatic negative effects on the lives of people worldwide. Globalization is a system or strategy that promotes worldwide application of economic policies, international security, health care and education, world indebtedness, and other issues formulated by dominant world powers. Globalization often perpetuates a widening gap between the rich and the poor within and between nations. As the powerful reap the benefits of wealth and prosperity, the poor have less and less. And the less economic power the poor have, the less access they have to institutions and systems that could assist them. Excluded by the effects of negative globalization, the poor live on the edges of materialism with despair as their basic commodity.

The world's women and children feel the negative consequences of globalization most forcefully. Global trade, dominated by a few economic powers, affects the ability of many developing countries to secure equal access to world markets. With power controlled by a few, many are excluded. Trade and industry profiteers frequently perpetuate low wages, degrading hiring policies, and abusive working conditions. Complaints or objections may lead to the loss of a job or to bodily harm.

The unequal distribution of wealth, cultural and environmental racism, interreligious tensions, and political instability bring new forms of exploitation, economic dependence, international debt, and greater impoverishment to large numbers of the world's population. Economic indebtedness has meant malnutrition and starvation, underinvestment in health care, and unequal access to effective medical treatment for the populations of most developing countries. Underinvestment in health care and overinvestment in international indebtedness challenge the prospect of a just social and economic development and a stable global security. Violence is a frequent response to these forms of injustice.

Industrialized countries cannot escape the consequences of economic exclusion. In the United States of America, the gap between rich and poor steadily increases. The poor experience segregation in education, housing, medical care, and community facilities. In the richest nation in the world, numbers of families live below poverty level with malnutrition that borders on starvation. According to statistics released in 2002 by the Children's Defense Fund, nearly 12 million children live in poverty; 4.6 million children live in extreme poverty; almost 13 million children live in families that do not get enough to eat. Complete lack of health care insurance is a reality for many of this nation's children, single mothers, lower-income families, and senior citizens. More than 9.2 million children (almost one in eight) have no health insurance. Infant mortality in the United States ranks 23rd among industrialized countries with 7.1 out of every 1,000 infants dying before their first birthday. Greed and unprincipled participation in exclusionary systems continue to make exclusion a form of injustice that isolates the human spirit and denies human dignity.

During the days of the judges exclusion was immoral and unjust, and it still is. If we find exclusion woven into the systemic web of power and elitism, then the possibility to resist exclusion is also woven there. Ruth affirms loving-kindness as the antidote to exclusion. Until those of us who call ourselves Christians repent and move beyond exclusions that we have tolerated, justified, or perpetuated, we cannot with integrity call ourselves the messengers of the LORD's loving-kindness. The message lived by Ruth and then preached by Jesus teaches us to love our enemies and to pray for those who hate and exclude us. For the sake of the world, we must keep trying.

Ponderings

Please take time to reflect on and ponder what you have read and studied in this chapter. The following questions and comments are intended to assist you. They may serve as discussion starters for group study, or they may be sources for contemplation and examination for individual use. Perhaps they will prompt further study and/or action. Through them you hopefully will bring forward the multifaceted meanings and implications of this chapter for living in our day and time.

1. Naomi complained that the LORD had turned against her. Arriving in Bethlehem embittered and wrapped in resentment, Naomi grumbled that she had returned "empty" and overlooked the presence of the one person who was devoted to her. The townspeople must have wondered what had happened to their pleasant, sweet Naomi of long ago. Naomi's bitterness affected her relationships and skewed her life perspective.

   - When has Naomi's refrain of "Why me?" been your refrain as well? When have you been overwhelmed with bitterness and felt that the LORD had turned against you?

   - What situations or events have caused you to overlook the presence of those who love you and commit to your care?

   - When you have felt "empty," where did you place the blame? How did that emptiness affect your relationships? How did you return to a sense of fullness? How did Ruth attempt to deal with Naomi's emptiness?

   - The role of martyr is an unpopular stance that often alienates those around you while attaining the desired results. When have you, like Naomi, taken on this role to get what you wanted? How worthwhile was the role in achieving your goal?

2. Ruth and Naomi were childless widows, the poorest of the poor. For widows, aliens, and others whose earnings fell below the poverty line, gleaning was the welfare system of Bethlehem and all Israel. Women in the United States are the fastest growing segment of the population confronting poverty. Elderly females, the mother roots and the wise grandmothers of this nation, constitute a higher percentage of the population of the poor than any other group. Married women often drop below the poverty line when a divorce or death occurs. A fast-growing population among the homeless are single mothers and other women, including elderly women. A life of poverty is increasingly the reality for many women.

   • How does this picture paint with accuracy the dilemma of women in your nation who become the recipients of charity or who struggle on less than subsistence income?

   • How might changes in economic practices, social security policies, and health care initiatives make you vulnerable to the reality of a life of poverty? What can you do to protect yourself and those you love from the "feminization of poverty"?

   • Ruth gleaned in the grainfields in order to provide food for Naomi and herself. In what ways do women who are caught in the cycle of poverty glean from someone else's prosperity in order to sustain their lives?

3. Ruth the Moabite was a foreigner who immigrated to Bethlehem. While immigration laws probably did not exist in ancient Israel, Hebrew laws favored one population and excluded others, including the Moabites. We may find similarities between Ruth's her-story and the debate in the United States of America about enforcement of its immigration laws. Pro-immigration movements support open immigration and welcome

immigrants as priceless resources while embracing diversity as a desirable strength and virtue. Anti-immigration movements favor one population and seek to halt immigration of outsiders.

- How do you respond to the belief that immigrants, refugees, foreigners, and political fugitives drain the economy, take jobs away from those within the country, and avail themselves of limited resources without contributing to society's welfare? What assumptions inform your response?

- How do you respond to the understanding of immigrants as priceless resources that strengthen national well-being through their diversity? What assumptions inform your response?

- What is your ancestral history? How is your heritage like or unlike that of foreigners and refugees who now seek a home within the borders of your country?

- What has been your experience with immigrants, refugees and other "outsiders"? How does the story of Ruth cause you to question your first impressions about such people?

4. Negative globalization occurs when a few nations control the world's economic and political resources. It effectively excludes developing countries from equal access to world markets and limits access to resources and systems that could assist them.

- Negative globalization as described in this chapter is a reality. What might be some of the positive benefits of globalization? How can positive globalization and its benefits become more inclusive and less exclusive?

- In our global village, what effects does globalization have on women whose situation of poverty and despair is akin to that of Ruth and Naomi?

- In what ways does globalization affect the lifestyle of you and your family? How might reading labels before you make clothing, food, and household purchases affect your buying decisions?

5. Ruth teaches us that we are connected to all creation through the Lord's loving-kindness; we are agents of one another's salvation—even our enemies and those who use us. Ruth the Moabite is remembered as a woman whose loving-kindness extended to others in ways that included and redeemed them.

   • How do you extend loving-kindness (action that goes beyond obligation, duty, or responsibility) to those who exclude you?

   • When has your "enemy" showed you loving-kindness? In what ways did that action surprise you? From whom do you withhold loving-kindness? For what reasons?

   • Jesus taught his disciples to pray for their enemies and for those who spitefully used them. How do you pray for your enemies? What is the difference between praying *for* your enemies and praying *about* your enemies?

6. On the journey to Bethlehem with Naomi, Ruth left all that was familiar: her god, her people, her customs and culture, her family and property. She willingly chose to go with Naomi without knowing what her future would hold in a strange land with a people she did not know and a foreign LORD to whom she had pledged allegiance.

   • When have you willingly left what was most familiar to you? What prompted your decision?

   • At that time what about your future seemed uncertain?

   • Leaving behind the familiar can be a risky emotional, spiritual, or physical journey, yet it provides an opportunity to get rid of "stuff" that holds us captive to what has always been. Even though you may desire changes in your life, what holds you back from taking the risk to move on?

What comforts and security are you willing to release in order to move on?

- Under what circumstances would you again choose to set out on a new journey and leave behind all that is now familiar to you?

- If you could choose one of the three female ancestors of Jesus we have studied to accompany you, whom would you choose and why?

7. Leaving the familiar changed not only Ruth's life but the lives of all she met. From her mother roots came Obed, David, and Jesus the Messiah, the "son of David."

- What impact has this study of Ruth had on your self-understanding?

- How are you like or unlike Ruth?

- How do you think Ruth would respond to your assessment? What will you do with your response?

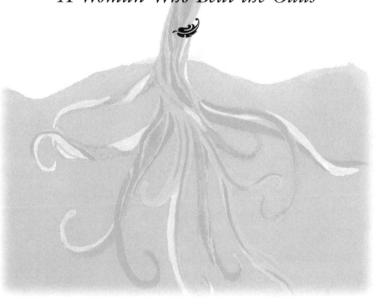

CHAPTER FIVE

BATHSHEBA

A Woman Who Beat the Odds

Before reading the chapter, take time to remember as much as you can about Bathsheba's story in the Bible. Recall all the details you can about who she was, her description, her relationships, and when and where she lived. Then read 2 Samuel 11–12; 1 Kings 1:11-21, 28-31; 2:13-21; 1 Chronicles 3:5; and Matthew 1:6*b*.

Locating the Story in the Bible

For Bathsheba's story to have full effect we need to understand the passages in Second Samuel and First Kings as a continuous narrative, reading First Kings in light of what we know from Second Samuel. To the writer of First Chronicles, David is the ideal king. Because the David and Bathsheba account in Second Samuel and First Kings casts David in a negative light, the chronicler does not mention it. The sparse verse in First Chronicles names Bathsheba as the mother of four children by David. Most scholars assume they are all sons, but this remains uncertain. Other than a recitation of genealogy, this verse has little bearing on the domestic life and political dynamics of the court intrigue that surrounded Bathsheba and finally led to Solomon's succession to the throne. The Gospel of Matthew (1:6*b*), which traces the genealogy of Jesus to David and on back to Abraham, refers to her as "the wife of Uriah."

Ask a Question—Get a Story

What about Bathsheba? Who was she? What do we really know about her? Why does Matthew's genealogy include her as one of Jesus' female ancestors? Can she find her way to us in her own right, or will she remain simply a beautiful attachment to the men who surrounded her? Will we ever hear her voice? What is hidden between the lines awaiting our discovering, uncovering, and recovering? What are we to remember about Bathsheba?

The Hebrew Bible tells us Bathsheba possessed great beauty and was the daughter of Eliam and the wife of Uriah the Hittite. She became a widow, pregnant with a baby conceived in an adulterous affair probably not of her choosing. She lamented the death of her husband and became one of David's wives after the mourning period for her dead husband. She suffered the illness and death of her first son and bore David four more children. One, a son named Solomon, became Israel's king, and was noted for his wisdom and power. From the moment King David first viewed Bathsheba in her ritual bath until the enthronement of her son Solomon, Bathsheba continued to be a woman of fierce tenacity, a woman who found ways to beat the odds. More than a survivor of King David's court, she became the first queen mother of Israel.

To learn any more about this ancestral mother of Jesus requires that we faithfully and prayerfully read between the lines of the text. To strengthen the bridge between Bathsheba and us, we must ready our spirits for the surprises present in the text's absences. We must prepare our hearts to be sensitive to the silence between the printed words and attune our ears to hear what remains unsaid in the gaps. We must open our eyes to what awaits us in the shadows with Bathsheba that wants to come into the light.

The First Turning: Remembering

It was the spring of the year, the beginning of the battle campaign season. At the end of the rain but before the heat became too great, kings and armies went out to do battle; but David did not follow the approach of most kings. David stayed in Jerusalem, and the biblical text does not tell us why. We do know that David sent Joab, his faithful general, with the officers of the royal bodyguard and all Israel to fight and ravage the Ammonites. "All Israel" probably meant the diverse conquered clans and tribes now considered part of Israel's domain.

The days in Jerusalem were hot, and David rested on his couch. One day in the late afternoon, David took a stroll on the roof of his house. The cool breezes usually blew gently at this time of day and refreshed the hot, oppressive air. Jerusalem, a former small-city capital of Canaan, was now a long, narrow city with a population of about twenty-five hundred. From the highest vantage point of his royal rooftop, David could see out across the city.

As he strolled and looked, David saw a beautiful woman bathing. In this dusty city openly bathing on a rooftop was a usual occurrence. Not immodest or socially indiscreet, the woman was actually performing a ritual cleansing as required by the religious law of Israel. She was purifying herself after her menstrual period (Lev. 15:19-24). Overcome by her beauty, David sent someone to ask about the woman. The answer came back that she was Bathsheba, the daughter of Eliam and the wife of Uriah the Hittite, who was presently serving in battle to keep secure David's kingdom. David sent messengers to bring her to him.

From the outset this story illustrates lethal love. Engulfed by lust and with full knowledge of her marital status, the king had sexual intercourse with Uriah's wife. While Joab ravaged the Ammonites, David ravaged Uriah's wife. Only David had the power to act on such a selfish whim. The balance of power tilted in his direction.

A woman subjected to the king's will, Bathsheba found it impossible to resist David. If the monarch wanted her, he would have her—and he did.

Then Uriah's wife returned to her own house as a polluted woman, made unclean by David's invasion of her body. Though the king himself had sent for her and molested her, if found out, Bathsheba would be subject to a charge of adultery. Guilt carried a sentence of death by stoning. Since the woman was usually blamed, Bathsheba knew what her fate would be. The wife of Uriah alerted David to the certainty of her conception with a brief and straightforward message: "I am pregnant."

Since her husband had been away in battle and Bathsheba had just finished the ritual cleansing after her period, doubtless the child she carried in her womb was David's. David had not figured Bathsheba's pregnancy into his selfish action; he could see the dark clouds of tragedy on the not-too-distant horizon. The exposure of his crime against Uriah could lead to his own death by stoning. Not even kings were exempt from the laws of Israel (Deut. 22:22; Lev. 20:10). His plan to cover his indiscretion did not include marrying Uriah's wife. The text does not indicate that he had any feelings of compassion for the woman or guilt about his actions. Nor does it hint that David took any blame or responsibility for the dilemma he had created. David was concerned for his own safety, that he not be caught. His life depended on it.

Immediately after receiving the message from Uriah's wife, David sent word to Joab to return Uriah the Hittite to Jerusalem. Uriah came to the king; and under the pretext of concern for Joab and all the people who were fighting, David asked how the war was going. The interview finished, David encouraged Uriah to go to his house and bathe his feet. While this was a standard Israelite custom, it was also a traditional euphemism for sexual intercourse. To entice Uriah even more, a present from the king followed him when he left the royal palace.

As one of the king's mighty men consecrated for war and blessed by a priest, Uriah had taken a vow to keep himself from all women during his active duty as a soldier (1 Sam. 21:4-5). Sexual relations with a woman were believed to rob a man of vitality, energy, and power to fight. Potency in bed before battle would lead to impotency on the battlefield. The soldier would lose his courage and virility and respond like a woman. Uriah had made a vow of abstinence that included Bathsheba, his wife. Instead of going to his house as David had ordered, Uriah slept at the entrance of the palace with the king's other servants and officers.

When David learned of Uriah's detour, he sent for Uriah and demanded to know why he had not gone down to his own house. Faithful to his soldier's vow, Uriah responded that as long the ark, the portable chest that contained the tablets of the law and housed the invisible presence of the LORD, was kept in a temporary booth and as long as the king's troops remained camped in the open on the battlefield, he could not—no, he would not—break his vow. He would not eat, drink, or sleep with his wife.

Intent on ensuring that Uriah slept with his wife so that David's adultery and fatherhood would not be found out, the king invited Uriah to stay another day. The two men ate and drank until Uriah was drunk, but still the soldier chose to sleep with the servants and officers rather than with his wife, Bathsheba. David behaved in a manipulative way; Uriah was straightforward and transparent. David's motivations were dark and wrong; Uriah's were honorable and right. Uriah was more righteous as a drunken soldier than was the deceptive and tricky King David when sober.

Uriah the Hittite's name meant "God is light," which suggests a probable conversion to Yahweh. The Hittites had settled in the land before the time of David, but under David's rule all the non-Israelite tribes and clans, including the few remaining Hittites, officially became "Israelites." Many adopted Hebrew names, as Uriah did. Yahweh, the LORD, became their god but not necessarily their only god. Many assimilated "Israelites" still engaged in god and goddess worship alongside their worship of the Hebrew LORD. The old rituals of their holy places and their daily lives changed little for most of these assimilated peoples. But the fact that Uriah had taken the Israelite soldier's battle vow of sexual abstinence suggests that he was more than a casual convert. Uriah, inflexible and single-minded, was a pious and committed man of integrity and fidelity to his king, his king's LORD, his general, and his comrades in battle.

Possibly court gossip about David and Uriah's wife filtered through to bodyguards inside and to soldiers outside the palace. Uriah may have been aware of David's crime against him and of the king's attempt to manipulate him into sleeping with his wife. If so, even without sexual intimacy, Uriah's presence in his own house with his wife could have served as public confirmation of his paternity. As one of David's "mighty men," Uriah knew from experience that the king obliterated any power but his own. Uriah knew as well that the refusal to stay with his wife meant his almost certain death. Nevertheless he would rather die with his honor intact than live his life as a compromising lie. And die he did.

Uriah carried his own death sentence in a sealed letter from the king to Joab on the battlefield. Positioned at the front lines in the heat of battle, Uriah was killed. David sent a callous message back to his general: "Do not let this matter trouble you, for the sword devours now one and now another." Little did David realize that his prediction would come upon his own household. He showed no sign of remorse at the death of one of his "mighty men" nor compassion for Uriah's wife, who was now a pregnant widow.

But Uriah's wife lamented the death of her husband. She

lamented that despite her youth, she was now a widow and pregnant. She lamented that her dead husband was not the father of the child she carried. Bathsheba had much to mourn, but whether her heart was truly broken or whether she was performing a mourning ritual, we do not know.

Becoming a widow, with or without a child, in the Israelite culture of that day placed a woman in a vulnerable, powerless, and frightening situation. Women gained status, power, or prominence only through the men to whom they were attached—a father, a brother, a betrothed, a husband, or sons birthed by them. A married woman had access to society through her husband, but a widow like Uriah's wife was at a social and economic disadvantage in her culture. This stigma probably would make Uriah's wife willing and grateful to marry any man who would have her.

With the mourning period over, David again sent for Uriah's wife. This time she came to him as an available widow. He expressed no concern for her situation or for the grief he had initiated through the arranged killing of her husband. Instead he evidenced only greed, self-gratification, and abuse of power. Taking Bathsheba as his wife was David's last chance to cover up his adultery. We are given no inkling of Bathsheba's feelings. Still known only as Uriah's wife, she became the wife of the man, albeit the king, who first had victimized her and then had had her husband conveniently killed. Now she would give birth to his child.

Not surprisingly the LORD was displeased with David because David had scorned the LORD, taking Bathsheba sexually while she was yet the wife of Uriah. The Bible consistently condemns adultery. The law of Israel should have protected Bathsheba as a married woman, but she dared not resist the king's desires. David's violation of Bathsheba became the turning point for the monarchy

—and with it, David, his family, and his kingdom began to unravel. The LORD was displeased with David, not Bathsheba, and did not condemn or judge her. But as the victim of David's sin, she suffered the consequences of his lust and power.

The LORD sent the prophet Nathan to confront the king. Nathan told David a parable about a rich man and a poor man. He intended to get David involved in the story—to convince David rather than accuse him. The rich man of the parable had many flocks and herds, but the poor man had only one little ewe lamb that was like a daughter to him. When the rich man needed to prepare a meal for a guest, he selfishly seized the poor man's only lamb and served it to his guest.

The hearing of this parable about the rich man's behavior greatly angered David. He pronounced the rich man deserving of death because he had showed no pity. David did not realize that he had just judged himself. He too had seized a lamb, the beautiful Bathsheba, another man's wife, and had done so without pity or compassion. Bathsheba had been nothing more than a beautiful ornament to be used to gratify the king's lustful desires. With no thought of consequences—until he was in a position to be caught —David had tossed the law aside to satisfy his own uncontrollable passion (Exod. 20:17).

Nathan announced that David was the rich man in the parable and spoke the LORD's scathing judgment on David. The LORD had chosen David to be the anointed king over Israel and had given more to David than he would ever need. But instead of showing gratitude for what he had received, David had despised and degraded the word of the LORD to do what was evil. Ingratitude and greed, even more than adultery, were David's sin. He had taken what was not his, and because David showed no pity for Bathsheba or Uriah, the LORD warned that trouble would come against him from within his own family. The sword would never depart from his royal household. To show no pity or compassion was to despise the LORD, which meant death for David.

Unable to deny his actions, David confessed his transgression and stood guilty before the LORD. Although the law of exact retaliation, *lex talionis*, was the way of the LORD and according to the law David should die, the LORD favored David by forgiving his sin. But the effect of David's evil could not be avoided. God's moral order would not be compromised—not even for a king. Beginning with the LORD's announcement that David's about-to-be-born innocent child would suffer and die, David's sin set off tremors that shook the entire kingdom. The king's relationship to God decided the relationship between God and God's people. Divine judgment required rectification. David escaped death; the child would not. With David's disobedience sin occurred; evil was done; and the innocent suffered and died. So the downward spiral began.

In a religious and cultural climate where children, especially sons, were deemed a blessing, the baby born to David and Uriah's wife almost seemed a curse. The unnamed son became critically ill and suffered greatly. While the child lived, David lay on the ground and prayed. He fasted and wept and pleaded with the LORD to take pity on him and let the child live. For whom did David pray—for himself or for the child? When the child died on the seventh day, David rose up, bathed, and changed his clothes. He went to the house of the LORD and worshiped and then to his own house, where he ate the food that was set before him. David's grief did not follow the traditional ritual of mourning. The meal he ate was not a funeral meal but his acceptance that the LORD's will had been done. The law of exact retaliation had been satisfied.

Only after David had performed his ablutions and other rituals following the child's death did he go in to console Bathsheba. David had been punished for his sin, but was not Bathsheba also punished? Did not David's great sin become Bathsheba's greater loss? Surely she experienced deep sorrow at the suffering and death of her first child. Her heart must have been broken. The text would have us believe that David and his grief were of paramount importance. (Only after the death of the baby conceived in adultery does the biblical text call Bathsheba David's wife.) Bathsheba was invisible and silent through what must have been a most tragic and lonely time. A brief notation of her suffering fails to relate the depth of her grief, entombed even as was her dead child. The text tells us only that the king finally comforted her, though we well may wonder if he comforted Bathsheba in order to receive comfort.

The story does not suggest that David loved Bathsheba or had any feelings for her, but we know he did lie with her again. Bathsheba conceived and bore another son, and the king named him Solomon. Connected with the Hebrew word *shalom*, this name meant peace, prosperity, and well-being. The LORD loved Solomon and sent a message by Nathan the prophet that the baby was beloved of God. The birth of Solomon opened a door for the creation of a new future for Israel. Despite God's displeasure with David, God's plan for Israel would prevail. Bereft of compassion from David, Bathsheba received the gift of God's compassion in the midst of tragedy, and from the ashes of chaos and sin fresh hope rose up. David's bloodline remained intact, the monarchy secure. Most important, Solomon, divinely designated to sit on the throne, would build the LORD's temple.

However, God's compassion did not rectify David's sin. For the rest of David's reign, the sword never departed his household. One violation led to another and yet another. What began in David's own household—fighting and feuds among kin, rape and family tragedies, lust and conspiracy, jealousy and murder, military intrigue and attempts at stealing the thrones of other kings—

spread like a malignancy throughout his kingdom. The aftermath of David's sin infected and affected the entire community.

Now an older, penitent king and a mere shadow of the powerful military strategist he once had been, David repented daily for the rest of his life for his scorn of the LORD and doing what was evil. As the years passed, David's sin took its toll. In his advanced years, David suffered chills, and his body took no pity on him. Even when covered with bedclothes, he never felt warm. His servants found a beautiful young virgin, Abishag the Shunammite, to wait on the king and to lie in his bosom and warm him. She stayed with David as his servant and royal concubine, but he was not sexually intimate with her.

During this unhappy time, David's oldest living son, Adonijah, proceeded to declare himself king without David's knowledge or consent. If David accepted Adonijah's claim to the throne and Adonijah chose a different prophet, Nathan realized that his own position as resident prophet to the king would be jeopardized. He would be banished or even killed. Bathsheba knew that Adonijah's claim to the throne meant that she and Solomon would be declared traitors. She could be exiled to the king's harem or worse, and Solomon would pose a threat to the throne. Both probably would be put to death.

With the possibility of banishment and death hanging over them, Nathan and Bathsheba conferred before they set in motion the plan to place Solomon securely on the throne. Nathan advised Bathsheba to go to King David and remind him that he had previously sworn to her Solomon's succession as king. Whether fictitious or real, that oath had proved to be of no consequence since Bathsheba was reminded that her life and the fate of her son depended on the changing whims of the king.

As advised, Bathsheba went to the king's chambers where the young and beautiful Abishag the Shunammite waited on the king.

An audience with David usually required an invitation from the king, but Bathsheba initiated this visit without invitation and not without risk. In her attending role, Abishag could hear and observe all that transpired. After bowing low in homage, Bathsheba made her request, embroidering the words Nathan had instructed her to say with more pointed words of her own. She noted that all of Israel awaited the king's announcement of his successor, and she integrated concern for herself and Solomon. In sympathetic tones she expressed understanding that the king would not want to die with a diminished reputation among all the people. Displaying intelligence, diplomacy, and discernment, Bathsheba reminded David that he had sworn by the LORD his God that Solomon would succeed him to the throne. He could make good his oath, or Solomon and she would be put to death by his silence.

In the meantime Nathan had arrived to confirm Bathsheba's words but found there was little left for him to say. Bathsheba had outspoken him! In the presence of his wife, the one whose name meant "daughter of an oath," David vowed that Solomon would sit upon the throne that very day. Having showed herself to be a woman of courage and some power during this exchange, Bathsheba must have been gratified by this positive and quick response. Perhaps she had engendered David's respect over the years and had become an influential presence at court. Whether David had at one time given Bathsheba his oath to have Solomon succeed him or whether she and Nathan simply took advantage of a senile king, by evening Solomon sat on the throne.

After the death of King David, Adonijah came to see Bathsheba, asking that King Solomon give him Abishag the Shunammite, David's servant, for his wife. Even though Adonijah had given up any pretense of claim to the throne, Bathsheba must have recognized the underlying threat in his request. She had a vested interest in keeping Solomon securely on the throne. After all the years of family betrayals and duplicity, perhaps she was ready to be rid of Adonijah's troubling presence. The cryptic silence in the narrative exposes little about the motives of Bathsheba or Adonijah, but it does invite questions and inference. Years ago Bathsheba had entered the court of King David a blemished woman in great shame. Now King Solomon greeted her with reverence. He rose from his throne, bowed down to her, and had a throne for her placed on his right side—a place of power and authority.

Bathsheba made her request on behalf of Adonijah to which Solomon reacted strongly. In ancient Semitic custom a dead king's concubines and wives, symbols of his political power and authority, became the succeeding king's possessions either by inheritance or by force. The man who possessed the women was the one who claimed the throne. Throughout the history of the Bible, women —whether mothers, daughters, wives, concubines, or harlots—had been handed down and back and forth. Power and authority, war and politics, tribal feuds and family disputes had been etched on the bodies and souls of women across the centuries. Solomon's biting reply acknowledged the political implications of Adonijah's request, which Solomon likened to a grab for the throne and the kingdom. As far as Solomon was concerned, Adonijah's request was tantamount to treason.

Adonijah would be a constant threat to Solomon and Bathsheba as well as to Israel's security. Abishag the Shunammite, whom Adonijah wished to marry, had overheard the previous negotiations among David, Nathan, and Bathsheba regarding the succession of Solomon. A liaison between Adonijah and Abishag would not be in the best interest of Solomon's rule. Immediately after the conversation between Bathsheba and Solomon, Adonijah was executed.

With Solomon firmly established as king, his mother, who helped secure the throne for him, exits the narrative. The story of Bathsheba in the Hebrew Bible ends as it began—without her voice or even her muted presence. The only other mention of Bathsheba comes in First Chronicles and in the genealogy of Jesus from the Gospel of Matthew. Bathsheba embodied beauty and dignity as she beat the odds to overcome tragedy and deceit. Through it all, she remained steadfast.

Her-story Embedded in History

The books of Second Samuel and First Kings are part of a unit of historical texts that have been called the "court history of David." The entire narrative also moves toward Solomon's accession to the monarchical throne. Together these two books form part of a larger work known as the Deuteronomistic history. In the books of Joshua, Judges, First and Second Samuel, and First and Second Kings, the Deuteronomistic editors and writers sought to preserve Israel's history from the time of the conquest of Canaan and the Promised Land to the Babylonian exile.

While the editors were historians who recorded Israel's history, the process did not follow contemporary critical-historical methods. The editors' primary concern did not center in the chronological recording of factual events. Their first intent was to unfold history as a revelation of God's moral order, to explain causes and effects in daily life, and to make sense of them in terms of God's abiding presence. They wanted to keep alive their understanding of who the God of Israel was and of the ways this God interacted with God's people throughout the history of Israel. The Deuteronomistic texts give us some idea of what was believed about God and what were the responses of the Israelites to God during the time of the court history and the succession narratives. We also see that the Deuteronomistic historians' ideas about God did not remain static. Even the God of Israel was on the move, refusing to be confined to a particular place or time or image or language.

The God of the Deuteronomistic historians was a gracious and merciful lover, a jealous and wrathful punisher—abundant love and consuming judgment at once. God forgave sin but also enforced divine retribution, which passed from one generation to the next. God's law was *lex talionis*—exact retaliation—with no compromise. Because David sinned, God's punishment was visited not only upon David but upon Bathsheba in the death of their son. Yet divine retribution did not erase David from the divine memory. David's sin did not cancel his place in the heart and mind of God, who continued to be with David through all.

David was the first monarchical king of Israel who was truly chosen and anointed by God. Saul, who had been king before him, had ruled through a combination of charismatic judgment and authority, but the LORD rejected Saul's kingship. As an institution, monarchy was a new concept of governance with David's accession. A clear system of succession had not yet been established, nor was it certain that David would choose a successor. Israel, being a small nation constantly threatened by larger and more powerful nations, survived through the trickery of the judges and kings. They claimed that their successful political schemes and battle maneuvers had been divinely inspired. David had refined both political and military tactics until they were an ingrained part of his personality, the framework of his private as well as public life.

In his old age David became sexually and politically impotent. The primitive belief that an aging male's sexual powers could be restored through contact with a young virgin and that political virility and vitality would accompany this restoration brought Abishag into David's life. His impotence, especially with the attention of this beautiful young virgin, became sufficient reason for his rivals to depose him. Impotency in bed signified impotency in politics and battle. All of David's surviving sons except Solomon plotted and conspired to take over the throne. One by one their presence was removed until only Adonijah and Solomon remained. Given this situation, David's designation and blessing of Solomon as his successor were extremely important; it left no doubt who was to be king. Solomon succeeded David to the throne by divine choice (2 Sam. 7:12-13; 1 Kings 3:11-14), but the road to the throne had taken many detours marked by knotty (naughty) family relationships and the threat of political upheaval.

The progression from a decentralized government presided over by charismatic judges to the centralized monarchy of David meant a change in the balance of power. The less stable environment of a decentralized power had given women more freedom to inherit, own property, hold public office, and even assume positions of cultic leadership. A centralized and inherited monarchy like David's tended to be more hierarchical and patriarchal. Men dominated both the political and family scenes. Inherited monarchy and other forms of inherited authority within the society passed from father to son. Women seldom occupied public positions of power and authority. Self-identity and self-determination were nearly impossible for women of Israel during monarchical rule.

The identity of women and what little power and control they could claim also depended on their family's connections to and intersections with those who held positions of power and authority. Women had to be cunning and solicitous in order to receive any benefits, freedom, and independence. This necessity was particularly true within a royal family. With no ruling power of her own, Bathsheba had to use her wits to derive even a small measure of power and public presence from the men who surrounded her.

The deeper meaning of Bathsheba's story is difficult to unearth because it is so firmly embedded in the court intrigues of David's reign. Bathsheba's calculated and risky involvement in ensuring

Solomon's succession is all the more astonishing in light of her gender and her membership in the royal household. Without Solomon as king, she would have had no power or prestige or prominence. In Solomon's reign, however, she became the queen mother and had a designated office with special duties, which may have included taking charge of King Solomon's harem. Bathsheba became the most influential and powerful female in all Israel.

We learn little about Bathsheba's her-story from the biblical text. The story in Second Samuel casts Bathsheba primarily as an object of desire to be dismissed and easily forgotten. Our lack of knowledge makes it difficult for us to relate to her. While necessary for plot development and important to the story's outcome, Bathsheba never develops into full personhood; the writer denies her any point of view or perspective of her own. This oppressive restraint is perhaps as devastating to Bathsheba's character as is the physical violence inflicted on her by David. Many biblical scholars, commentators, and preachers have targeted Bathsheba as the reason David's private and public lives begin to unravel in chaos. Not given the freedom to defend herself, Bathsheba is charged with seduction and adultery.

Other than the brief, poignant message to David about her pregnancy, Bathsheba is mute during the early part of her-story. We never learn what she thinks, how she feels, or how self-conscious she is about her situation. Seen only through the eyes of the writer and David, she remains a vessel for what they choose to initiate through her. They control not only her but what we know about her as well. She is the pawn, never the player.

No longer satisfied to be acted upon, Bathsheba in First Kings defines her own terms of being. She becomes a visible subject and an active participant in the life of the court; we experience the evolution of her personality from helpless victim to dignified survivor, from the shame of adulterous pregnancy to the honor of queen mother. Through slight hints about her emotions, concerns, and motivations, we learn enough to discern that she is a real person who now earns respect from the men who surround her. Although speaking only when prompted by men to do so, Bathsheba shows she can hold her own—even with the king. She has found her voice and uses it to secure not only her future, but the future of Solomon and thus the future of Israel as well. Bathsheba matures into a forceful and clever presence at court, astute at political maneuvering and adept at turning opportunities to her advantage. She exerts her influence directly and becomes a catalyst through which significant events happen. While the story may not be about her, she emerges from David's shadow as the one person to whom Nathan and Adonijah bring their requests and to whom both King David and King Solomon defer.

Second Samuel portrays David as the self-assured, calculating king who grasps for women and kingdoms that are not his. Bathsheba remains the powerless, abused victim of royal power. The reversal of First Kings is explicit. In the end David can no longer grasp for anything. His political and sexual powers decline; he is impotent both on the throne and in bed. Even as David's power and influence diminish and wane, Bathsheba's power and influence flourish and grow. Bathsheba's increased confidence and resourcefulness lay the groundwork for Solomon's accession to the throne and for lasting changes that benefit all Israel.

The Second Turning: Reading between the Lines

Over the centuries of largely male scholarship and religious patriarchy, Bathsheba has most often been portrayed as temptress and chastised as adulteress. From this perspective Bathsheba's guilt was not that she bathed but that she was seen. Being seen was the foreplay to possession. She made David do it by allowing herself to be seen. The man could not help himself; she wanted to be possessed. Her beauty, which stoked David's unbridled lust, somehow made her more guilty and David less so. A common observation is that flaunting her body was an act of flirtation, and washing herself in plain view of the king was both an invitation and an explanation for the royal rape that ensued. Bathsheba wanted to be seen; she asked for and deserved what she got. In fact she should have been honored that the king sent for her and brought her to the palace.

Such an interpretation deftly shifts to Bathsheba the responsibility for the consequences of David's actions. One scholar has said that before Bathsheba we see "David under the Blessing"; after Bathsheba we witness "David under the Curse," blaming her for what David would not or could not control within himself. We collude with David and the writer when we characterize Bathsheba as a paragon of temptation and sexual desire. Such a stereotype invites women and men to accept the false claim that the female gender is the source of man's temptation, the fundamental reason for the downfall of otherwise good men.

All of us are called to set aside what we think we already know as truth and to make ourselves available and vulnerable to her-story in new ways. All of us are challenged to read between the lines self-consciously, to acknowledge our personal agenda, to recognize cultural biases and religious prejudices, and to take responsibility for our own interpretations. Unless we meet this call, Bathsheba will remain the victim of constricted theological imaginings.

Women's Rights Are Human Rights

In Bathsheba's her-story who is in a position to use and abuse power? Who possesses enough power to override/ride over those with less or no power? In the succession narrative of Second Samuel we find a repeated use of the word *send* or one of its related forms. David *sends* for Joab his general. He *sends* for Bathsheba, and he *sends* for Uriah the Hittite. He *sends* messages, and he *sends* others to do his will. He asserts his power, and his sending gets the intended results. David has the authority to send for or to send away, and he uses his liberty to do so frequently.

Regardless of the details and circumstances surrounding Bathsheba's bathing, David the king has the power to send, to act on his desires for or against someone. The patriarchy of ancient Israel meant male entitlement that most often led to possession. This ancient attitude, upheld by religion, culture, and tradition, remains a contemporary issue the world over. Now as then, women and children are victimized and traumatized because of power struggles initiated by men who hold the power to *send*. Often the women and children are the innocent and powerless recipients of abuse by the world's military contingencies, governments, and religions. Tradition and authority still reside with men who determine life and death through their power to give orders.

We have made progress, but the reality of equal human rights for women has a long way to go. While a number of countries have prohibited discrimination on the basis of gender, INTERACT, an Amnesty International USA bulletin about women's human rights, concluded that "women are still treated as second class citizens all over the world." It reported that by the end of the twentieth century two-thirds of the world's millions of illiterate people were women, that women continued to bear the double burden of work and child care while earning and owning less than men, and that they had little access to forums that make decisions about their bodies and about society's organization and governance. Persons in authority with the power to stop injustice are the same ones who benefit from keeping the status quo.

In every armed conflict, civil war, and act of genocide, women and children experience brutal and persistent violence through rape, torture, and murder without impunity. International human rights organizations increasingly recognize the practices of honor killings, bride burnings, female genital mutilation, forced prostitution, forced pregnancies, and domestic violence as violations of a woman's rights. Many women, like Bathsheba in Second Samuel, have been emotionally traumatized and sexually violated. They live every day and night in fear and remain the silent victims in a no-win situation of life or death.

To avoid violent acts against their person, some women become refugees, fleeing from governments and families that are unable or unwilling to protect them. Many female refugees are victims of torture, abuse, or some form of sexual assault. They are often afraid or unable to articulate their experiences to men in uniform or the immigration authorities. In their attempt to escape persecution, these women are least likely to have valid documentation of their status and proper papers that prove their identity. Until recently, the United States government often did not recognize women in this situation as refugees who qualified for asylum, returning them to the countries they had fled where they faced torture, imprisonment, and almost certain death upon their return.

In December 2000, the United States Justice Department and the Immigration and Naturalization Services (INS) published new regulations to cover women's asylum cases. Even with "friendly" regulations, women's refugee claims and appeals remain before the Bureau of Immigration Appeals (BIA) for months, often years. Indifference within the INS/BIA to the plight of female refugees remains a cause of great anxiety and fear of those seeking asylum.

At the heart of Bathsheba's her-story then and women's her-stories now, war, politics, religious upheavals, patriarchy, and possession continue to be etched on the bodies and souls of women. The quest for domination, regardless of the consequences, is with us yet as an evil that still greatly displeases the LORD.

Ponderings

Please take time to reflect on and ponder what you have read and studied in this chapter. The following questions and comments are intended to assist you. They may serve as discussion starters for group study, or they may be sources for contemplation and examination for individual use. Perhaps they will prompt further study and/or action. Through them you hopefully will bring forward the multifaceted meanings and implications of this chapter for living in our day and time.

1. Bathsheba, the female ancestor of Jesus, took risks. She evolved from being a victim of the king to becoming the most influential woman in all Israel. Bathsheba encourages women today to say no to power and authority, government and military tactics that use and misuse them and to say yes to self-identity and self-determination.

    • Name women you have known who took risks and "beat the odds" of adversity, tragedy, and family divisions. What do you admire about them? How have these women encouraged you to take risks?

    • When have you had the conviction to take a stand against persons, organizations, or systems that have mistreated and disregarded you as a person of value? When have you chosen your own path? What were the results?

    • What would happen if more women, along with protesting past and current restrictions and inequalities of imposed cultural/social/religious expectations of women, together worked vigorously toward the vision of a future they want for themselves and generations yet to come?

2. David sinned and acknowledged his sin. God modified the consequences of sin for him, but others still suffered, including Bathsheba and her baby son. God never condemned Bathsheba,

but she reaped the consequences of David's actions—an innocent baby was struck ill and died.

- The story interprets sin as having cause and effect. What life experiences support this interpretation for you? Based on your answer, how do you describe the consequences of sin?

- What in David's actions disturbs you? When have your thoughtless or careless actions brought about suffering for innocent people? When have you lacked pity and compassion in your relationships? What did you do?

- What will you do to become more aware of how and when your actions might cause negative consequences and pain for others?

3. One of the ageless truths about the narratives in the Hebrew Bible is that they help interpret us to ourselves. Three of the main characters (David, Bathsheba, and Nathan) can inform us about who we are or are not. Reading the story with a contrite spirit, we may better understand our own human frailties.

- When you yield to temptation and use whatever power you have to manipulate others to get what you want—even when it is not yours to get—how can you identify with David? What can David teach you about this kind of manipulative behavior? How would you change this behavior?

- When people see only your outward appearance and miss who you really are, or when they expect you to stay in your place and keep silent, how can you identify with Bathsheba? What have you learned from Bathsheba about this kind of situation? How would you change your situation?

- When you witness an unjust action and courageously speak out against it, how can you identify with Nathan the prophet? How does Nathan illustrate creative ways both to acknowledge and correct injustice?

4. The ancients of David and Bathsheba's time believed in a jealous God capable of capricious anger. Their God demanded retaliation for a sin committed—an eye for an eye, a tooth for a tooth, and a death for a death. This concept of retribution is called *lex talionis*. Some countries continue the practice of *lex talionis* in their justice systems.

   - What aspects of your society and religion implicitly or explicitly perpetuate this kind of in/justice?

   - What incidents of *lex talionis* have you experienced? When have you really wanted to "get even," to see someone else get "theirs"?

   - When have you found yourself making a *lex talionis* judgment that another person or group of people got what she/he/they deserved?

5. Some scholars and commentators blame Bathsheba for causing David to commit adultery. They would punish her for what David could not or chose not to control within himself.

   - When a woman is portrayed as the source of a man's temptation, what are the consequences for the woman?

   - In situations of domestic violence, date rape, and forced rape, what seems to be the prevailing attitude of many police officers, judges, juries, media reporters, and people in general with regard to these situations?

   - Where do you witness positive changes in attitudes and laws? What changes do you think still need to be made?

6. Rather than make uninformed judgments about how poor and desperate women secure their survival, perhaps we might investigate what is being done to break down the barbaric and uncivilized institutions and systems across the world that per-

petuate injustice, forcing many women to flee their situation or take justice into their own hands.

- What will you do to express your concern about the abuse of human rights of women and children globally? locally?

- How can you relate Bathsheba's position in David's court to desperate women who take justice into their own hands?

7. Bathsheba's story in Second Samuel portrays her as mute and voiceless. Dominated and controlled, Bathsheba seems to accept the identity David projects on her of the woman she should be. By allowing David and the other men who surround her to define her, Bathsheba never emerges as the full-fledged human being to whom First Kings introduces us.

- In what ways might Bathsheba have allowed herself to be defined by David's expectations? What other choices might she have pursued?

- In what situations does it seem easier for a woman to accept the male-projected identity than to refuse it?

- When have you allowed yourself to be defined by your spouse's or significant other's views? by your friends' desires for you? by the church's definition of what a woman should be and how a woman should act?

- How do your culture, class, or status define for women what is acceptable or unacceptable?

- When have you refused your identity as defined by someone else or something else? What did you learn about yourself? about others?

8. Bathsheba suffered personal tragedies and court betrayals as the wife of King David and the mother of King Solomon. Yet with steadfastness and unrelenting tenacity, she became a

woman of power and influence. Bathsheba is remembered as one of the female ancestors of Jesus the Messiah.

- What impact has this study of Bathsheba had on your self-understanding?

- How are you like or unlike Bathsheba?

- How do you think Bathsheba would respond to your assessment? What will you do with your response?

CHAPTER SIX

MOTHER ROOTS
Tracing the Family Tree of Jesus

THE FEMALE ancestors of Jesus have been our companions as we have made our journey through this study. We had to dig deep to find their mother roots, but find them we did. From between the lines of the biblical texts and the spaces and silences between the words, these women came to us. They stood in the gaps with us and reminded us that what storytellers leave out is sometimes just as important as what they include.

As we continue to trace the matriarchal family tree of Jesus, this chapter will look at places where the lives and personalities of Tamar, Rahab, Ruth, and Bathsheba may have intersected the life and ministry of Jesus the Messiah. Perhaps we will find some imprints left by these women on Jesus' path as he grew into his messiahship. We may see evidence of their transparent presence in the way Jesus related to others. Traces of who they were might even be revealed in the causes of justice and redemption Jesus embraced and for which he gave his life. Perhaps we will discover that the markings and signs they left along the way guided and inspired Jesus as he taught and healed and challenged the status quo of authority, tradition, and self-righteous religion.

Surrounded by their empowering witness, you will want to give yourself time to reflect on what you have learned from each of the ancestral mothers. What have they taught you about who they were, who you are, and how you feel about your own mother roots? Take time to remember Tamar, Rahab, Ruth, and Bathsheba; and in your remembering, be thankful.

Locating the Story in the Bible

We find the her-stories of Jesus' female ancestors in the Hebrew Bible. The ancient sages and rabbis deemed these women worthy by giving them a lasting place in the midrash of Judaism. Earlier chapters mention some of the sayings of the sages and rabbis with regard to these women. Many more traditions abound. In this section you will find more reflections about each of the ancestral mothers that have come to be part of the oral and midrashic tradition. Perhaps these perspectives will be yet another avenue for your coming to know better and experience these women.

The Genesis account supports one of the midrashic traditions about Tamar. When she was clearly pregnant but without a husband, she faced with great perseverance the accusations and adversity thrown at her. People knew that her husband was dead and that Onan, her brother-in-law, had refused to fulfill the levirate law. When confronted with the accusations that she had become pregnant through prostitution, Tamar would rub her swollen belly as she proudly replied that she carried within herself kings and redeemers. In the LORD's time this prediction was fulfilled. In another tradition Jewish sages seeking to interpret the zodiac calendar according to Jewish history and tradition rather than by the astrologers' art identified the twin sons, Perez and Zerah, of Tamar and Judah as the twins of the zodiac.

Midrashic tradition views Rahab as one of the four most beautiful women in the world. She is first a sinner, then a proselyte who became the wife of Joshua, and finally a prophetess who was the ancestor of prophets. According to one tradition, when Rahab told the spies none of the men of Jericho had any courage left (Josh. 2:11), what she really meant was that they had all lost their sexual potency. Rahab knew this because there was no prince or ruler in the land whom she had not known sexually. Rahab was ten years old when the Israelites left Egypt, and during the forty years they wandered in the wilderness, Rahab practiced harlotry. At age fifty, her life changed. She met two young Israelite spies and became an Israelite proselyte. She confessed her sins to the spies, and because of her redeeming actions in helping them escape, Rahab asked to be forgiven. An old rabbinic tradition had Joshua marry Rahab. She gave Joshua only daughters, but from these daughters descended ten priests and one prophetess.

The rabbinic literature credits God with incomprehensible power to choose and use righteous people from throughout the world. The LORD justified peoples and individuals through their righteousness, not their ethnicity or religion. Because Rahab, a non-Israelite, helped the LORD's chosen people enter the land of Canaan, she became a prototype for all those who consciously or unconsciously, through their own righteousness, obeyed the divine will. The LORD searched for those who belonged to the world and asked why they did not approach him. If they replied that they were sinful and ashamed, then the LORD responded that they were no more so than Rahab, who received robbers and prostitutes in her house. The LORD's loving-kindness was confirmed when the lost heard that Rahab approached the LORD in her sinfulness, and not only did the LORD accept her but prophets and righteousness came from her. If the LORD would do this for Rahab, so would it be done for those who belonged to the world but who also were righteous.

The sages believed that in the first conversation between Ruth and Naomi, Naomi's part of the conversation had been left out, so they used midrash to fill in the gaps. Midrash has it that when Ruth told Naomi she would go with her wherever she went, Naomi replied that Jewish women would not go to certain places like circuses and theaters. Ruth replied, "Where you go, I will go." Then Naomi informed Ruth that she (Naomi) could never live in a house that did not have a *mezuzah*, a small piece of parchment inscribed with a biblical passage, rolled up in a container, and affixed on the door signifying to everyone that a Jewish family lived within. Ruth replied, "Where you lodge, I will lodge." Ruth proclaimed that Naomi's people would be her people and Naomi's God would be her God. What she really meant was that she would leave the idolatry of Moab behind and depend only on the LORD God of Israel.

Midrashic tradition states that Boaz was first attracted to Ruth because of her modesty. The other women gleaners pulled up their skirts when they bent to pick up the grain; when Ruth gleaned, she knelt and kept her skirt down. The others flirted and engaged in coarse banter with the men who harvested the grain, but Ruth kept to herself and always acted demure. Many of the rabbinic scholars clearly affirm that nothing improper or unseemly happened between Ruth and Boaz on the threshing floor, which did not mean that Boaz had not been tempted. Boaz refused to give into temptation and did not lay a finger on Ruth. He remained steadfast in this commitment until he took counsel with the elders at the city gates and until he and Ruth were wed. Deuteronomy states that no Moabite can become a member of the Israelite community for ten generations. Then how could Ruth become the great-grandmother of King David? the sages asked. Their answer was that the Torah said Moabite and not Moabitess (the term used in earlier Bible translations to designate a female Moabite). Therefore Ruth as a Moabitess was welcomed into the community.

Midrash confirmed the strong relationship between Bathsheba and her son Solomon. The sages believed that Bathsheba was unique among and separate from the other wives of King David. In rabbinic tradition Bathsheba told Solomon that she was the only one of his father's wives to know his presence after she became pregnant. Wanting her son to have his father's looks and strength, she forced her way into David's chambers and slept with him while she carried Solomon in her womb. On another occasion Bathsheba told Solomon that the other wives of King David prayed that their sons might become king, but Bathsheba prayed that her son might love and study the Torah so that he would become wise as a prophet. Thus when the LORD later asked Solomon what gift he wanted bestowed on him, Solomon chose wisdom, having learned from the example set by his mother. The ancient sages described Solomon as the wisest of all human beings. He knew three thousand stories for every verse of scripture and over one thousand interpretations for every one of the three thousand stories.

Ask a Question—Get a Story

Do you remember the ancient rabbi's advice about reading the scriptures? "Turn it and turn it again, for all is contained in it," he said. We have turned the her-stories of Tamar, Rahab, Ruth, and Bathsheba over and over again, but you probably still have questions about them and their situations. Keep asking questions as we read this chapter. Here are some "starter" questions to consider:

How might the mother roots of the female ancestors of Jesus be entwined and tangled, as together they animate and quicken the growth of Jesus' family tree? According to the doctrine of the Christian church, because Jesus was conceived by the Holy Spirit, he is not related to these four women by blood or genetics, but possibly Jesus could have taken in something of their character and learned from their strength in the same way that we learn from generations past. Persons often refer to this way of knowing as "received knowledge" and "collective unconscious knowing." What could Jesus, by and through faith and unconscious knowing, have inherited from his ancestral mothers to assist him in his ministry? What knowledge might he have received from their her-stories?

The First Turning: Back to the Roots

Tamar became pregnant by her father-in-law. Rahab was a prostitute and a traitor, Ruth an enemy who practiced loving-kindness. Bathsheba's beauty prompted the ravishing of her body by the king. While these characterizations may be true, they tend to minimize and discount the important place given Jesus' ancestral mothers in the salvation history of Israel. Simplistic understandings do a disservice to their memories and to the depth and richness of their her-stories.

This study has intended to uncover and make accessible the mother roots of Jesus the Messiah. We have spent time with each woman's her-story and read about each woman's contribution in securing the Davidic lineage through which Jesus' messiahship is deemed true. We have come to know the women individually, but surely the mother roots in such a family tree branched out to entwine and tangle around each other. This section challenges us to search for the connections among these four women and to discover what they might have in common. Rooted in ancient and fertile soil, each mother root of Jesus searches out the others, and together they grow down deep.

REMEMBERING THE MOTHER ROOTS OF TAMAR

As the mother of Perez and Zerah, her twin sons by Judah, Tamar is the first in the entwined mother roots of the Jesus tree. Denied rightful access into her father-in-law's tribe, Tamar refused to be refused. She made his-story into her-story through an illicit sexual encounter with her father-in-law, Judah, an act so close to incest that many clergy, Christian educators, parents, biblical scholars, and commentators over the centuries have not known what to do with Tamar's story. (Similar frustrations abound concerning the sexual adventures of Rahab, Ruth, Bathsheba, and others in the Hebrew Bible.) Despite attempts to ignore Tamar or to explain Tamar's her-story away, Tamar still refuses to go away or to be left out.

The Bible records that Judah claimed the twin sons birthed by Tamar as his legitimate sons. Perez and Zerah were given all the privileges of inheritance and birthright that the patriarchal system allowed. While some modern commentators have called this "legitimated illegitimacy," the ancient Jewish sages and rabbis wrote that Tamar acted in accordance with the LORD's will and bore within her womb the divine seed. Persons in some Jewish circles viewed her as a paragon of virtue. Through the Holy Spirit she had saved Judah's tribe from extinction. As one of the supporting mothers of the Twelve Tribes of Israel and as the mother of Perez, whose lineage moves forward to King David and Jesus the Messiah, she deserves our homage. Rather than timidity, Tamar chose temerity. Her backbone and fortitude enabled her to act with courage and boldness, and she is rooted beside Rahab and Ruth, two other non-Israelite women with "chutzpah."

Tamar and Rahab the Canaanite prostitute (who practiced her trade during the time of Joshua) turned an unexpected moment offered to them into an opportunity that changed their lives and the lives of others. In curious and unconventional ways, the so-called trickery of Tamar and the lies of Rahab were their means of being faithful and obedient to the LORD. Tamar's moment of mistaken identity with Judah beside the road resulted in a pregnancy that enabled the tribe of Judah to continue and flourish. Rahab the prostitute hid the Israelite spies as she chose to use trickery and lies to defend and preserve Israel over against the king of Jericho and her own people. Convinced that Israel's LORD was above and below all and because of her faith in this LORD, she worked to help the Israelites gain the Promised Land.

Both Tamar and Rahab interceded on behalf of others. Tamar preserved the tribe of Judah, and Rahab saved her family and opened up the land of Canaan to the Israelites. A crimson cord symbolically binds them together. At the birth of Tamar's twin sons, the midwife tied a crimson cord around Zerah's wrist when he thrust his hand out of the birth canal, marking him as the first-born. Remember the crimson cord that Rahab hung in the window of her house as a sign for the Israelite soldiers during their siege on Jericho? The tradition of the ancient Jewish sages records that the two young spies saved by Rahab were Tamar's twin sons, Perez and Zerah, and the crimson cord that hung from Rahab's window was the same crimson cord that the midwife had tied around Zerah's wrist at his birth.

From the story of Ruth and Boaz we know that Tamar's birthing of Perez to Judah was already accepted in the Israelite tradition as one in which the LORD was involved. Boaz announced he would fulfill the obligations of a redeemer by acquiring Ruth, Mahlon's widow, "to maintain the dead man's name on his inheritance, in order that the name of the dead may not be cut off from his kindred and from the gate of his native place." The people at the gate and all the elders answered, "Through the children that the Lord will give you by this young woman, may your house be like the house of Perez, whom Tamar bore to Judah" (Ruth 4:12).

Both Tamar and Ruth were non-Israelite widows of Hebrew men. They needed a male relative to fulfill the levirate law or act as redeemer in order to secure their places in the house of Israel. As we discovered in Ruth's her-story, an intimate relationship with Boaz took place on the threshing floor before their marriage. Ruth married Boaz, who through the tribe of Judah was a descendant of Tamar. Rahab was Boaz's mother. Ruth was the mother of Obed, the father of Jesse, and Jesse was the father of David. As his great-grandmother, Ruth was the founding female ancestor of the House of David.

The lineage according to Matthew's Gospel is thus:

Tamar begat Perez and Zerah of Judah

Rahab begat Boaz of Salmon

Ruth begat Obed of Boaz

Obed begat Jesse

Jesse begat David

Bathsheba begat Solomon of David

Tamar and Ruth also had in common similar uses of clothing to cover themselves and further their own purposes. In the brightness of day Tamar veiled her face and draped her body and waited for Judah. In the darkness of night Ruth put on her finest dress and covered herself with a cloak and waited at Boaz's "feet" for him to wake. The clothing they wore hid their identities until the appropriate and opportune time. Both Tamar and Ruth did what they could to change the course of events for their own lives. Their actions ensured the succession of God's chosen people and changed the course of Hebrew history. Jewish and Christian scholars have taken notice of the other Tamars named in the Bible. Most conclude that they are probably the namesakes of this courageous ancestor of David the king whose her-story was written into history. King David's beautiful daughter was named Tamar (2 Sam. 13). She was Absalom's favorite sister, and after her rape by Amnon, her brother, she lived a life of solitude in Absalom's house as a "desolate woman." Absalom had his brother murdered for his crime against his sister and later named his own daughter Tamar. She was also a beautiful woman (2 Sam. 14:27). The text never mentions her again. If the conjecture of scholars is correct, the name of Tamar, first given to that magnificent and stately Canaanite, was carried forward victorious into the next generations with respect and reverence.

REMEMBERING THE MOTHER ROOTS OF RAHAB

The roots of Rahab the Canaanite prostitute go down deep in the fertile soil from which the family tree of Jesus grew. Enmeshed with the mother roots of the other female ancestors is Rahab's unique contribution to Israel's history: She lied for the faith to preserve God's covenant people and opened the way by which Israel gained entrance into the Promised Land. As a prostitute Rahab was an independent woman who provided for her own needs. She answered to no husband and went about freely without the usual restrictions placed on a married woman.

The drying flax on Rahab's rooftop suggests she was a spinner and weaver of linen. Rahab hid the spies beneath the flax, and the ancient rabbinic sages connected her with those families who made and furnished King David with the finest of linens. From the linens spun by Rahab, the curtain of the Ark of the Covenant and the tent of the Holy of Holies supposedly were made. In Rahab's day the spinning of cloth was considered a symbolic gesture of bringing forth, creating a new thing.

The symbolism of spinning soon became part of Israelite culture to articulate the idea that something new had come into existence with the emergence of Israel as a nation. Just as the LORD spun out new destinies from human fabric during the settlement period in Canaan, so Rahab spun out of her faith a new destiny for those Israelites returning from Egypt. Her faithful actions challenged Joshua and all Israel to adjust their attitudes about who was chosen and deemed worthy to dwell with them. While Joshua was alive, the Israelites lived in obedience with a new understanding of righteousness and a sharpened clarity of direction as the chosen people.

Rahab's willingness to be vulnerable is a characteristic that connects her to Tamar. Both were foreigners who found the Israelite culture and religion alien. But because they had a fierce faith in a God not their own, both willingly risked everything so that the LORD God could bring about something new through them. In Perez, one of the twin sons she bore by Judah, Tamar gave birth to the ancestor of David. Although some ancient Jewish sages write in their midrash that Rahab married Joshua and gave birth to daughters, the tradition cited in the Gospel according to Matthew names Rahab as the wife of Salmon, an Israelite who was the father of Boaz. However, fastening a date to Rahab as the mother of Boaz is problematic since the conquest of Canaan was nearly two hundred years before the time of Boaz. Yet most scholars conclude that Matthew meant that Rahab the prostitute was the mother of Boaz who married Ruth from Moab. Their son Obed bore Jesse, the father of King David. Through the Davidic line, both Tamar and Rahab claim their place in the matriarchy of Jesus of Nazareth.

Rahab and Tamar knew they could depend on no one but themselves. Undeterred by tradition, they adapted to the unexpected and chose a new life in a moment's notice. Tamar the trickster and Rahab the traitor acted deliberately and authoritatively as they defied their culture's moral laws in order to uphold and sustain what they perceived to be a higher purpose. Each woman did the wrong things for the right reasons.

In order to fulfill the levirate law of inheritance, Tamar broke another tribal law, becoming pregnant by her father-in-law Judah. But the breaking of this law fulfilled a higher purpose—the preservation of the tribe of Judah and a place in the house of Israel for Tamar. Rahab wanted to live and to save her family from destruction, but more important, she desired to give herself to Israel's LORD. Choosing life and sustaining her faith, she lied. She betrayed her king and her country in order to fulfill the desires of her heart. In her betrayal and lying, a higher purpose was served—her obedience opened the way for Israel to enter the land of Canaan.

REMEMBERING THE MOTHER ROOTS OF RUTH

Rich and moist, the grainfields of Moab were the first home of Ruth's tender roots. When transplanted to Bethlehem's soil, Ruth sought to put down roots in the grainfields of "the house of bread," where she hoped to glean. Embedded in Israelite soil, the tendrils of Ruth's roots sought and found the roots of the other female ancestors of "the Son of David" and bore the fruit of loving-kindness. Intertwined but with separate identities, the roots of Tamar, Rahab, and Ruth were strong and vital. Life flowed through them to restore the family tree of Israel, whose branches grew and flourished, until at last they came into full bloom in the wondrous birth of Jesus the Messiah.

The book of Ruth is filled with departures from customs and rules: the exceptional bond between two women; gleaning behind reapers while bundles still stood in the field; the "bridal" preparations to attract Boaz; the strange night on the threshing floor; Boaz's negotiations with the nearest kinsman; the exchange of the sandal that departed from the Deuteronomistic tradition; the reversed order of the townspeople's blessings on Ruth and Boaz; and the naming of the child by the women of the town. All these events were exceptions, outside predictable routine and customs. And Ruth was at the center of them. With her own "just intent" (as the Hebrews described her actions), Ruth takes her rightful place beside the other unconventional and bold women in the family tree of Jesus.

Ruth and Tamar, both initiators, acted as agents of change in their particular situations. Both challenged the stereotype of the childless widow in Israel and refused to remain in their mother's/father's house after being widowed. Both had male relatives who should have helped them, either through levirate marriage or redemption, but who seemed reluctant to do the right thing. Taking their reproductive future into their own hands Ruth and Tamar engaged in questionable and uncustomary conduct. Although by very different means, they both "uncovered" a man who gave them a son to perpetuate their dead husbands' inheritance. Their sons rescued the family lineage, which had been threatened. Through unconventional "uncovering," a recovering of the family was assured. While Ruth and Tamar trusted in Israel's LORD, they also helped make things happen.

Tamar's first intent was to see that justice was done, that she receive what was lawfully and rightfully hers. Ruth's first intent was to provide for her mother-in-law through the redemption of family property and lineage. Judah recognized the righteousness of his daughter-in-law Tamar and pronounced her more righteous than he. But Naomi had no final words of gratitude for Ruth who received from Boaz recognition and appreciation for her loving-kindness and loyalty. Perhaps Ruth's courage reminded Boaz of his own mother, Rahab. The LORD recognized Tamar and Ruth, for they conceived and perpetuated the family tree. And both served as models of loyalty to the Israelite community and to its LORD. May we esteem Tamar and Ruth, who overcame the insurmountable, determined their own futures, and guaranteed their security in the household of Israel.

Naomi, Boaz, the elders, and the women of Bethlehem all expressed their faith in the LORD. But Ruth, like Rahab, pledged loyalty to Israel's LORD only once. In her profession of belief to the young Israelite spies, Rahab acknowledged that their LORD was the God in heaven above and on earth below. In her oath of loyalty to Naomi, Ruth pledged that Naomi's God would be her God. Once Rahab and Ruth had spoken their loyalty and had placed their future with the LORD, being faithful to their pledge was all that mattered to them. Nothing more is written about their conversion to the way of the Israelites' LORD, yet their actions proclaim more loudly than words their faithfulness and loving-kindness. In choosing the LORD, Rahab sacrificed her city and the people of Jericho to save her family from destruction, and Ruth sacrificed returning to her family and homeland to save the continuity of a family not her own. Both women lived their lives boldly as if they knew the LORD had already blessed them and with the assurance that they would be redeemed.

Ruth, Rahab, and Tamar all were intercessors. Although their motives may not always have been pure, they consistently acted on behalf of others. In their refusal to accept the status quo, they transformed their situations. They were righteous and loyal foreigners who voluntarily chose to join themselves and their futures to Israel and to the LORD. While their bloodlines were "tainted" with intermarriage, they stood in stark contrast to many of their Israelite contemporaries who claimed pure bloodlines but whose actions were "tainted" with disobedience and disregard for the LORD's loving-kindness. Courageously moving beyond the traditional boundaries and prescribed behavior of patriarchal Israel, these female ancestors of Jesus changed and transformed the future of all Israel, thus the future of Christianity. We dare not take lightly these female ancestors of Jesus, for as their heirs we are rooted in their faithfulness to the LORD and their dedication to make a better world.

Ruth, Tamar, and Rahab were not redeemed because of their virtue and exemplary behavior. As outsiders they reminded the Israelites that the LORD often chose the very ones whom the people of the covenant thought were unworthy of redemption. The LORD came to the forgotten, the lost, and the least and used them to bring about the LORD's redemptive purposes in the world. These female ancestors prodded Israel to remember that in its failure to recognize the despised, the enemy, the foreigner, and the outsider as agents of the LORD's redemptive activity, it had failed to remember its own history of alienation.

God frequently had to remind the Israelites that they were once outsiders who had no home and no land, that when they were no people, the LORD adopted them and made a nation out of them. The LORD heard their cries not because they were righteous but precisely because they were outsiders with no future and no hope. The LORD took pity on them, bestowed loving-kindness (*chesed*) on them, and redeemed them from themselves. These ancestral mothers remind all Israel and each of us that not our faithfulness and loving-kindness but God's faithfulness and loving-kindness bring about our redemption.

For ever so long, silence has been the universal keeper of family secrets locked away in fear. The Bible family, like any family, wants to keep silent and buried any hint of illicit sexual relationships, especially incest, and most especially in the lineage of Jesus. But embedded in scripture and among the entwined roots of the ancestors, the family secrets are right there for all to see. Ruth was descended from an incestuous coupling between Lot and his older daughter. Boaz descended from a sexual encounter between the too closely related Tamar and her father-in-law Judah. Rahab the prostitute was certainly far from pure and virginal. While Bathsheba may have been more victim than willing participant, she nonetheless lived with the consequences of an adulterous sexual liaison. Yet from these forbidden sexual encounters were born Perez, Obed, Jesse, David, and Jesus. Whether we like it or not, it is all there in the Hebrew Bible. Regardless, the Bible used by Christians proclaims that these enigmatic sexual unions gave to the world the Savior of all creation.

Remembering the Mother Roots of Bathsheba

As the wife of David and the mother of Solomon, Bathsheba takes her rightful place in the family tree with the other female ancestors of Jesus, her roots interwoven with the mother roots of Tamar, Rahab, and Ruth. When David did not have a son who could inherit both his own kingdom and the kingdom of Saul, Bathsheba gave birth to Solomon. Years went by, but at the critical and crucial time for David's successor to be decided, Bathsheba reappeared. With her persuading influence, Solomon became king, the monarchy established by David continued, and David's royal bloodline was secured and passed on through the generations to "Jesus the Messiah, the son of David, the son of Abraham" (Matt. 1:1).

Bathsheba performed the ritual bath of purification after her menstrual period, either as an Israelite or as a faithful Yahwist convert, according to the Mosaic law. While the writer does not state that Bathsheba was an Israelite, we do know that she was the daughter of Eliam, whose name in Hebrew means "God of (the) people." Eliam could have come from a conquered tribe or clan, adopted a Hebrew name, and become a Yahwist convert, as Uriah the Hittite apparently did.

The biblical text tells us that Bathsheba's son was named Solomon, although it emphasizes that the Israelite prophet Nathan sent a message from the LORD to name the child Jedidiah. Perhaps the name given was not thought good enough for King David's son. Yet Solomon is the name that remains in the pages of the Bible and is remembered by both Jewish and Christian believers.

Some commentators support the conjecture that Bathsheba also was the granddaughter of Ahithophel the Gilonite, whose trusted royal counsel to King David was like an oracle of God. Information found in 2 Samuel 23:34, where Eliam, the son of Ahithophel, is named one of David's mighty men, fails to certify that either of these men was related to Bathsheba. Regardless of her lineage, Bathsheba was married to Uriah the Hittite. In itself, this act of intermarriage (if she was an Israelite) may have set her apart from the Israelites who kept the bloodline pure by refusing to intermarry with foreigners.

Although Bathsheba becomes more real to us as the biblical narrative moves along, she also remains somewhat distant and out of reach. Because few clues are given us, we have little understanding of the journey she took from being Uriah's wife to becoming the queen mother. Even in the company of the other female ancestors of Jesus, she continues to be a foreigner to us. These other great women all have a voice and tell their own stories, while Bathsheba has to struggle to speak—to find her voice and make it heard. They make decisions on their own behalf and without any prompting from the men who surround them, and from the beginning of each of their stories we get some idea of what they think, how they feel, what they want, and how they plot to get it. But Bathsheba reveals herself to us at a slower pace and less completely as she makes her way from being an object of beauty acted upon to a new self-understanding where she acts with authority on her own behalf.

Bathsheba and Tamar form their own alliance within the family tree of the ancestral mothers, having at least two things in common: (1) they both had husbands who did evil that displeased the LORD and caused the women to suffer as innocent victims, and (2) they both embodied feminine traits about which men were suspicious or uneasy. Tamar's first husband Er "was wicked in the sight of the LORD, and the LORD put him to death" (Gen. 38:7). Onan was Tamar's second husband: "What he did was displeasing in the sight of the LORD, and he put him to death also" (Gen. 38:10). The biblical text tells us that "the thing that David had done displeased the LORD" (2 Sam. 11:27). After Bathsheba and David were married, he acknowledged his sin and was told, "the LORD has put away your sin; you shall not die. Nevertheless, because...you have utterly scorned the LORD, the child that is born to you shall die" (2 Sam. 12:13-14).

Er, Onan, and David discovered that sin carried with it a price tag. Where disobedience occurred, sin resided; punishment followed, and often death resulted. While both Bathsheba and Tamar suffered the consequences of their husbands' sin, God did not hold the women accountable and strike them down. Tamar experienced the death of her husbands and Bathsheba experienced the death of her firstborn son, but God never condemned either. Yet by association both of them can tell us much about sin and its effects.

Israelite patriarchy revered and feared the unexplainable and mysterious power of women as bearers both of life and death. Bathsheba and Tamar shared this perceived power. Judah knew that after his two oldest sons went in to Tamar they died. In his mind the obvious effect of intercourse with Tamar was death. In the intimacy of sexual relations Tamar had the power to deliver death as well as bear life, a mysterious force that Judah could not explain. Judah's fear of Tamar caused him to breach the levirate law by sending his daughter-in-law, while betrothed to his third son, back to her father's house as a shamed, childless widow. He took this action and ignored the unsandaling ceremony that would have released Tamar from the levirate bond and given her the freedom to marry again.

For the Israelites blood was the source of life and death, having the power to cleanse or pollute. It was a source of good or evil, and the taboo associated with women's blood and its flow from the body was powerful as exemplified in Bathsheba's her-story. Although the Israelites suspected a tie between a woman's menstrual cycle and conception, the biological facts had not been clearly established. Because they had no explanation, they considered menstrual blood to be suspect and impure as well as life-giving. Thus the culture confined a woman to a separate place in her home during her menstrual flow. After a woman's menstrual period, she performed a ritual bath, a *mikvah*, in order to make her clean and pure again. The flow of blood and its related power were so mysterious that if a man had intercourse with a woman during her period and before her ritual bath, he would be made unclean (Lev. 15:19-24). Indeed there was power in the blood.

Perhaps more than any of the other female ancestors of Jesus, Bathsheba personally experienced the effects of a culture that understood blood as a source of evil. Her suspected rape and the murder of her husband by David, the death of her first son, the raging violence between David's sons—their betrayals and murders, the rape of David's daughter Tamar—were a constant "bloodbath." Yet Bathsheba's roots refused to be cut off or stunted. They grew steadfastly and quietly as they found a rightful place among the other roots of the robust and essential female ancestors of Jesus.

Her-Story Embedded in History: An Inheritance by Faith

Each of us is born into inextricably interwoven kinships, community systems, and global infrastructures that connect us with all humankind—past, present, and future. Each of us inherits a complex private, social, and cultural collective consciousness from external sources and from authorities with which we can identify. Yet beyond this conscious knowledge may reside a reservoir of inherited collective unconsciousness that remains largely unknown but awaits discovery.

Because our individual stories are deeply embedded in history and traditions that extend across many centuries, generations, and cultures, all of us unconsciously know more than we think we know. Because we have acquired and received knowledge and accumulated wisdom from ancient and modern sources, all of us can do and be more than we consciously think. Inherited memories from sources beyond our knowing link us to all generations of humankind. And because we are surrounded by so great a cloud of witnesses, all of us have received an inherited faith that first lived in our ancestors and now lives in us. Through them more of God's spiritual nature has been passed on to us than we can ever imagine or intuit. We cannot fully grasp this kind of collective knowing by rational means only. It comes to us through faith. Perhaps Jesus had this same experience. Luke's Gospel tells us that Jesus increased in wisdom, in years, and in favor with God and people (2:52).

Perhaps things essential were imparted to Jesus through the faith of his female ancestors, through communion with their witnessing spirits. This connection possibly made Jesus at ease in his healing and life-giving relationships with women of all stations and ages. Perhaps the collective memory Jesus received from his female ancestors empowered him to live beyond the acceptable cultural boundaries with integrity and boldness. Their faith lived again in Jesus as testimony of God's extravagant mercy and loving-kindness.

The radical love and obedience Jesus first witnessed in his mother's life still are spinning out justice and transforming the world. Just as surely as each ancestral mother's story is rooted in the other biblical stories, all their her-stories are embedded in the story of Jesus— the one to whom their lives pointed. What Jesus inherited through the faith of his female ancestors may be as strong a witness to his messiahship as any biological inheritance.

The Second Turning: Reading between the Lines

TAMAR AND JESUS

As an adolescent Jew, Jesus studied in the synagogue, where he memorized the names of the patriarchs, prophets, and others who played a role in the salvation history of the Israelites. Sitting with the family circle for high holy days and numerous special occasions, he probably followed the custom of the ages as he recited and rehearsed the list of generations, which included his ancestors. Israelites believed that the souls of the dead resided in Sheol for eternity and should not be forgotten. To be remembered through lineage was the only life after death the ancient Hebrews believed they would have.

When the genealogies were recited, Jesus probably heard the name of Tamar called out along with Rahab, Ruth, and Bathsheba, and perhaps their inclusion in that long roster of the faithful piqued his curiosity. He grew up hearing stories from the Hebrew Bible and the elaboration of these tales by the rabbis. As a young boy Jesus probably listened intently to the adventures of Tamar, a unique story among the genealogy of the patriarchs and kings. Perhaps he heard the rabbis raise questions about Tamar's behavior, while in the same breath upholding her as a virtuous and righteous woman. And if we look closely, we may comprehend Tamar's authority, intelligence, and artful maneuvering stamped on the life and ministry of Jesus. No one knows when and where the Spirit blows; but across the mysteries of time and space, Tamar surely breathed into Jesus her passion for justice and righteousness as well as her radical determination to see situations through.

Righteousness in the Hebrew Bible came about through right relationships: just, true, and faithful. It insisted that a person treat others the same way in which he or she wished to be treated. Until a person established a right relationship with the LORD he or she could not be in right relationship with anyone else, even the stranger who sojourned with the Hebrews. In a society of right relationships, no one was to be left out (Lev. 19:18; Lev. 19:34; Deut. 6:5). Tamar understood right relationships more from the heart than from the law, and she sought to hold Judah accountable for his relationship with her and to make it right. Maybe this female ancestor impacted Jesus' life when he chose to live in right relationship at some risk to himself and when he called his disciples to moral and ethical living.

Jesus stayed in trouble with religious authorities. After a series of incidents in which the chief priests, scribes, and elders had tried to trap him through his words, he affirmed the commandment to love one's neighbor as oneself above all others (Mark 11:15–12:34). The religious leaders of his day found Jesus' challenging interpretation of the law unacceptable. Like Tamar Jesus used unconventional means to make his point as he lived what he believed to be the truth. His parables confused and frustrated the chief priests, scribes, Herodians, Pharisees, and elders and relentlessly trapped them with their own logic and words. He cleverly countered their deception, as Tamar had done centuries before in dealing with Judah's deceit and wrongdoing. Perhaps this style of repartee came naturally to Jesus through his knowledge of Tamar.

One time the scribes and Pharisees brought before Jesus a woman who had been caught in the act of committing adultery

(John 8:2-11). Intending to test Jesus with the hope of bringing charges against him, they asserted that according to the law of Moses the woman should be stoned to death. Perhaps as Jesus bent to write on the ground, he remembered that Tamar, one of his great-grandmothers, had been sentenced to be burned alive for the same sin of adultery. Perhaps he envisioned Tamar standing before Judah saying, "Pay attention. Take note, for I am with child by the man to whom the seal, cord, and staff belong." Maybe it was Tamar's name that Jesus wrote in the dust with his finger.

Jesus knew that what motivated Judah centuries before and what now motivated the scribes and Pharisees was self-interest. Judah, the chief religious authority of his tribe, wanted to get Tamar out of the way. Now before Jesus stood the religious authorities of Israel who wanted to get him out of the way. But like Tamar who was not ready to die, Jesus knew his time was not yet. Perhaps also remembering Judah, who when confronted publicly with his sinfulness had confessed his own guilt and turned away, Jesus straightened up and said to the elders, "Let anyone among you who is without sin be the first to throw a stone at her." When they heard this statement, they confessed their own sin as one by one they dropped their stones and turned away.

Tamar was one of the first women in the Bible to practice outright civil disobedience. Her sense of social responsibility and keen consciousness of justice redeemed not only herself but also the tribe of Judah. Her life embodied the justice that transformed, causing systems and institutions to bend and people to change. In her attempt to hold those in authority accountable according to the ancient Hebrew laws, Tamar defied the social and moral codes of her day. Her determination to see wrongs made right caused a reversal of roles. Powerful Judah became vulnerable and weak, while powerless Tamar took on strength and authority.

Jesus deftly used role reversal in dealing with those in power.

Perhaps Tamar's example enabled him to master this strategy of confrontation, to use the deceptions of the patriarchal structures of Jewish law to show the value of all persons—including women. Throughout his ministry Jesus exhibited Tamar's passion for justice and compassion. He consistently disregarded the social and moral codes of first-century Palestine in order to meet human need. He touched those who were unclean—including women. On the Sabbath he healed the sick—including women. He was called a drunkard and a glutton, a friend of tax collectors and sinners—including women. (Read Deuteronomy 21:20-21 for punishment related to drunkenness and gluttony.)

Jesus spoke to women in public and listened to their concerns. This deep sense of social responsibility rooted in the commandment of love got both Tamar and Jesus in trouble. Their civil disobedience countered the religious traditions and cultural structures that oppressed and prevented some people from attaining the freedom promised them by the LORD. They undid the power of injustice, bringing redemption to others, and undid the power of death as they chose the power of life and new beginnings. They risked scandal for the possibility of right relationships. Perhaps Tamar's outrageous courage infused determination into Jesus' being when in the garden he pledged to see his journey through to the end, wherever and whatever that might be.

RAHAB AND JESUS

From Jesus' encounter at age twelve with the teachers in the Temple, we know that all who heard Jesus were amazed at his understanding. A wise and thoughtful child, surely also curious and inquisitive, he confidently asked questions of the teachers in the Temple. Perhaps he directed questions about his family's heritage and Israel's history to Mary and Joseph as well. Maybe he asked about Rahab the Canaanite prostitute to whom he was connected.

Although Rahab was a woman of uncanny insight, we may wonder how she knew what she knew about her faith in Israel's LORD. She had not been taught, but she perceived the truth. Like Rahab, we do not comprehend for certain how we came to know all that we understand about the truth of collective ideas or emotions. Are we mysteriously linked to our ancestors, who from their graves teach us yet? Perhaps such a possibility existed for Rahab and Jesus too.

What enabled Rahab to grasp the truth that life involved more than a strict keeping of the letter of the law? Turning over the Israelite spies to the king's men would have kept the letter of the law, but Rahab savored the "spirit" within the law. And so did Jesus, who lived by the spirit of the law. Perhaps he thought of Rahab when he ate with sinners and tax collectors or when he spoke to women in public and ignored the cleanliness laws for the sake of human need or let a sinner wash his feet with her tears and dry them with her hair. Perhaps Jesus remembered that Rahab had loved God with all her heart, soul, and strength, and that she also had cared for enemy spies and her family. Might memory of Rahab have prompted Jesus to add "Love your neighbor as yourself" to that first great commandment from Deuteronomy 6:5?

Jesus might have learned something about God's everlasting and healing love from Rahab who had already lived what Jesus would teach—that God's love is unconditional and no one ever deserves or merits the extravagant outpouring of God's gifts. God gives to the righteous and the wicked. Our challenge comes in receiving those gifts without reservation and giving thanks for them through obedient living. Perhaps Rahab's story reminded Jesus once again that God does not wait for us to become perfect before acting through us, in us, and for us. God waits for our response and then, like Rahab, we not only receive blessings but become a blessing to others.

During his life and ministry Jesus persistently challenged the hypocrisy of religious authorities. After entering Jerusalem among cheering crowds and cleansing the Temple of the money changers, he cured the blind and the lame and cursed a fig tree because it was without fruit. Asked by the chief priests and elders by what authority he took these actions, he answered, "Truly I tell you, the tax collectors and the prostitutes are going into the kingdom of God ahead of you" (Matt. 21:31). Perhaps Jesus silently called the name of Rahab the prostitute, his ancestral mother, as he spoke to those who had no room in their hearts for such despised outsiders.

This prostitute, from whose roots the seed of Jesus grew, exemplifies another of Jesus' teachings. Peter complained that the disciples had left everything to follow him, and Jesus assured them they would follow him into the kingdom of heaven. He said, "At the renewal of all things...many who are first will be last, and the last will be first" (Matt. 19:27-30). Jesus might have thought of Rahab, who surely was last by the standards of her culture, when he spoke these words. Yet the epistles of Hebrews and James name Rahab first in the faith. Unlike Nicodemus the Pharisee, Rahab knew what it meant to be born again (John 3:3-4). In her new relationship with God, she was no longer last but first, and the promised kingdom would be hers.

The fathers of the early Christian church showed a particular interest in Rahab. They taught that Rahab's name in Latin was *latitudo*, which means breadth and range, freedom from the usual restraints and regulations. Free from the restraints and regulations of her culture, Rahab the prostitute extended the breadth and range of Canaan to include Israel. Like the Israelites who marked their doorposts with blood to escape the avenging angel of the LORD, so Rahab hung the crimson cord in her window to safeguard her family from destruction. Similarly, the early fathers interpreted Rahab's her-story as a foreshadowing of the crucifixion of

Christ and of the future of the early church. Through the symbolism of the crimson cord, Rahab was deemed the prophetic witness to the blood of Christ, the Paschal Lamb, that yet was to be shed on the cross.

Like most of us, Rahab had lived much of her life unaware of the full consequences of her actions. Yet when holiness entered her life, she experienced God's liberating presence. This unexpected gift of freedom turned her around, and perhaps she saw herself—really saw herself—for the first time. From the darkness of her existence and all that had been, she welcomed the empowering presence of the Holy. From Rahab's old self emerged a new being.

Perhaps as Jesus hung on the death-tree planted by his enemies, Rahab's presence hovered nearby. In life her faithful actions had worked to free and redeem others. In death her faith might still have been working, pouring over Jesus like a balm of Gilead. And Jesus, breathing deeply, inhaled the liberating presence of God. With the promise of new life yet to be experienced, Jesus embraced holiness.

RUTH AND JESUS

The story of Ruth was beloved by the ancient sages of the Hebrew faith. Jesus probably was taught in the synagogue about her loving-kindness. He also must have known that her Moabite lineage and status as an outsider excluded her from the assembly of the LORD. Perhaps with his knowledge of Ruth's her-story Jesus began to form his own understanding of the LORD's inclusive loving-kindness (*chesed*) and of the risks involved if he were to live it out in his life.

Jesus knew that exclusion sometimes led to violence. Perhaps in telling the parable about a good Samaritan who helped a wounded Jew on the Jericho road he remembered Ruth's caring for others as a good neighbor (Luke 10:25-37). Samaritans, deemed less worthy by the Jews than even a Gentile, were excluded from the Israelite community because of their intermarriage with foreigners. Jesus knew a story about any Samaritan would be difficult for his listeners to comprehend. They would question how an outsider, beyond the covenant and despised, could possibly be an instrument of their redemption and salvation. Perhaps the spirit of Ruth the Moabite inspired Jesus as he told the story, witnessing to the truth as he spoke his challenge: to the neighbor whom you excluded and counted out, show mercy and loving-kindness. Go and do.

Jesus's behavior during his encounter with the Canaanite woman in the district of Tyre and Sidon, when he seemed to forget about neighborliness, mercy, and loving-kindness (Matt. 15:21-28), may puzzle us. The woman begged Jesus for help, and he at first responded with silence. Then he insisted that because he was sent only to the lost sheep of the house of Israel, he (a Jewish Messiah) should not take the children's food (teachings of salvation) and throw it to the dogs (the Gentiles). Perhaps the memory of Ruth pricked Jesus' conscience and enabled him to see that the fullness of his ministry and mission went beyond the Jews. In turning to reward the Canaanite woman for her faith, Jesus turned as Messiah toward the whole world. Ruth and the Canaanite woman reminded Jesus—and they continue to remind us as Christians— that God's concern extends beyond those who see themselves as favored and securely tucked under the shelter of God's wings. In God's realm of right relationships, all have a place of honor.

The loving-kindness and loyalty that Ruth pledged to Naomi were extraordinary. Because of her commitment Ruth left everything familiar—her father and mother, her people and country, and her security in a god she knew—to join her life with that of a powerless widow who had little security to offer, not even a place to lay her head nor food for the next day. Perhaps Ruth's example of compassionate faithfulness and uncompromising commitment stirred in Jesus' mind when he said to his disciples, "Whoever loves father or mother more than me is not worthy of me" (Matt. 10:37). To the crowds who followed him Jesus said, "Whoever comes to me and does not hate father and mother, wife and children, brothers and sisters, yes, and even life itself, cannot be my disciple" (Luke 14:26).

Without position or power, Jesus depended on the goodwill and hospitality of others for food and lodging. He was marginalized by those in authority, and some questioned the legitimacy of his birth. Yet Jesus and Ruth teach us that although we cannot save ourselves, we are called to be agents of one another's salvation. What others would have us keep secret God uncovers, uses, and redeems. Ruth and Jesus both display the redemptive strengths that make manifest the wholeness and near presence of God.

The deep level of friendship shared by Ruth and Naomi rarely finds an equal in the Bible, although David and Jonathan's devotion to each other's welfare may run a close second. The men's love moved beyond the logical and explainable. At Jonathan's death David lamented, "Your love to me was wonderful, passing the love of women" (2 Sam. 1:26). Perhaps loving deeply and extravagantly ran in the family of Ruth, David, and Jesus. At the Passover supper in the Upper Room, the disciple, "the one whom Jesus loved" (John 13:23), reclined next to Jesus (some say that he rested his head on Jesus' bosom) while Jesus talked about friendship and love. Jesus commanded his disciples to "love one another as I have loved you. No one has greater love than this, to lay down one's life for one's friends" (John 13:34-35; 15:12-17). A short time later in a lavish giving of self, Jesus laid down his life for his friends.

God blessed Ruth with loving-kindness, enabling her to love her enemies. Her loving-kindness extended beyond predetermined boundaries; she leveled the walls of nationalism and prejudice and pointed to the future when God through Jesus the Messiah would pour out love that had no human bounds. Jesus might have seen in Ruth's example the redeeming love that embraces excluded ones and restores them to abundant life and joyous living. From the roots of Ruth, whose name meant "beloved companion and friend" came Jesus, whom the whole world has come to know as a beloved friend and companion.

BATHSHEBA AND JESUS

Surely Jesus heard stories about Bathsheba when he went to the synagogue to be taught by the rabbis. Through the experiences of Bathsheba, his ancestral mother, he might intuitively have known and understood many things about his own identity and calling. If we open ourselves to the possibility of this mysterious and unexplainable way of knowing, we may see Bathsheba's imprint on the life and ministry of Jesus. Standing with the cloud of witnesses that surrounded him, Bathsheba was present and available to Jesus.

Bathsheba experienced all the restrictions in the Mosaic law associated with blood taboos and uncleanness of women. Jesus, who had learned the laws of Moses and had been raised to be a good Jew, knew about the power of blood and the taboos associated with it. Yet when Jesus encountered the hemorrhaging woman, he set aside the levitical cleanliness laws that had kept this suffering woman separated from the larger community for twelve long years (Matt. 9:20-22; Mark 5:25-34; Luke 8:43-48). Her touch did not offend him nor was he concerned it had made him unclean. Instead he called attention to the fact that she had touched him and that her faith—not his—had made her well. Choosing love and healing to meet human need, Jesus restored the woman's rightful place into the fellowship of the Israelites by calling her "Daughter," perhaps recalling the honored memory of another "daughter" of Israel, Bathsheba.

Perhaps Bathsheba's experience moved Jesus better to understand that the power of beauty, if used for righteous purposes, could be the generativity needed for a spiritually transforming experience. In his own ministry Jesus upheld the right and appropriate place of beauty in the disciplined life of discipleship. Jesus knew that blindness to God's presence in and through the revelation of beauty in all its forms—reducing beauty to mere human terms—can lead to brokenness, alienation, violence, and death. For Jesus expressions of God's truth, goodness, and mercy were interwoven through the verities and textures of beauty.

The story of the woman who anointed Jesus with expensive oil confirms his appreciation of beauty. The woman's extravagant action disturbed the dinner guests, probably male, who harshly belittled her. But Jesus chastised them, affirmed the beauty of her actions, and praised the woman for what she had done. Receiving her attentive gift with pleasure and gratitude, he applauded her deed by announcing to the guests that she had done what she could (Mark 14:8)—she did what she had the power to do. Jesus called this anointing a fine and beautiful thing, one of the good works (Matt. 26:6-13; Mark 14:1-9).

Jesus knew the need for fine and beautiful things; without them his followers would stagnate and become apathetic and listless. Having missed Jesus' point Judas sought out the chief priests in order to betray Jesus. The revelation of beauty in and through the woman's healing touch and gentle care as she anointed Jesus became the backdrop for what followed. Her beautiful act gave way to the violence of conspiracy, suffering, and crucifixion.

Bathsheba understood the suffering of the innocent in silence and the effects of sin not her own. She knew firsthand about use and abuse of power, which left no place of refuge. Perhaps what Jesus came to know about sin and suffering through Bathsheba helped prepare him for the loneliness he felt in the garden and as he stood in silence before Pilate. Perhaps the spirit of this ancestral mother embraced him on the cross when he felt forsaken, upheld him in his suffering, and finally welcomed him when the consequences of human sin took his earthly life.

Women's Rights Are Human Rights

When women do not receive equal justice and are treated as objects by those who make life-or-death decisions about their lives, the possibility of violence always supersedes the regenerative empowerment of women. Amnesty International's global Campaign against Torture reports that a woman is battered every 15 seconds in the United States, and 700,000 are raped each year, often by husbands, fathers, other relatives, employers, or neighbors. Often victims do not report abusive treatment because they fear for their lives or for the lives of their children.

Amnesty International has called upon the United States government and all world governments to protect women from violence in their homes, communities, and in prison. *Abuse of Women in Custody: Sexual Misconduct and Shackling of Pregnant Women*, a comprehensive report by this organization, addresses the specific issue of human rights for women in American prisons. This report documents state by state sexual abuses and ill treatment suffered by women prisoners. Each of the fifty states' policies and practices that enable these abuses also are outlined. Less than half of state prison systems meet Amnesty's human rights standards for safeguarding the protection of women prisoners. While some states have no laws protecting women prisoners from sexual abuse, other states hold a female prisoner responsible for sexual contact with a prison official. A number of states permit prison officials to restrain pregnant women during labor and delivery with humiliating devices, including handcuffs, leg shackles, and belly chains. Not only are minds and spirits shackled, but during this moment of giving life, bodies are also shackled.

The devaluing of women too often translates into discriminatory actions against them. Behind prison walls across the world abide the present-day contemporaries of Tamar, Rahab, Ruth, and Bathsheba; they feel trapped and cannot escape the discrimination that shapes their very existence. Attempted suicide in prison is a common occurrence. Safety behind the prison wall is a myth, and most women prisoners cannot assert themselves effectively for their own protection. Most seldom have a voice and speak up only at great personal risk. We are charged to pay attention to these women; the denial of women's rights anywhere casts a long shadow on human rights everywhere.

Ponderings

Please take time to reflect on and ponder what you have read and studied in this chapter. The following questions and comments are intended to assist you. They may serve as discussion starters for group study, or they may be sources for contemplation and examination for individual use. Perhaps they will prompt further study and/or action. Through them you hopefully will bring forward the multifaceted meanings and implications of this chapter for living in our day and time.

This study has emphasized the gaps and silences in the biblical texts as rich treasure to be mined for further understanding of the biblical narrative. You have been encouraged to read between the lines to hear the unspoken possibilities and challenged to use your imagination to ask questions of the biblical texts. You can apply the process used to delve into the depths of the her-stories of Tamar, Rahab, Ruth, and Bathsheba to your own story. To remember your life's narrative, to search for God's presence in and through it, is a spiritual practice in which you now are invited to engage.

Author and educator Sue Monk Kidd has suggested that we are stories being told by the divine Storyteller and that we knead our stories into bread so that we might feed one another on our journey. Indeed, the stories of our lives are sacred texts, and they are just as true and valid as are the stories of the female ancestors of Jesus. Each of us is a living historical document from which our story unfolds every precious minute of our lives. Like our lives, our stories are always in transition, in truth never-ending. We have our place in past and future genealogies. Our stories do not die with us, for they reveal what is most valued and sacred to us. They continue to nourish others, providing food for the journeys of our children, grandchildren and generations beyond, relatives, friends, and perhaps even for people we will never know. The promise of

Israel's LORD and our God is that even after death, we still are stories being told by the divine Storyteller.

1. Find a quiet place and a block of time. If not now, covenant with yourself to do so sometime in the near future. After you have settled into your surroundings and quieted your heart, take some time to remember the narrative of your life.

    *   Who are your mother roots?

    *   How did you find out about the roots from which you sprang? How deep are these roots?

    *   When have they been bread for your journey?

    *   From what other sources or storytellers did you learn about your journey and your identity?

2. Read between the lines and through the empty spaces of the unique sacred text that is your life. Probe the gaps and silences to hear what remains unspoken or forgotten. What waits in silence or lies dormant is just as revealing as what you choose to remember and tell.

    *   From what kind of soil did you grow? How did it foster and sustain your growth?

    *   What questions do you still have about your roots and the soil that grew your family tree?

As you remember the narrative of your life, you may realize that God did not save you from susceptibility to the consequences of bad choices and embarrassing mistakes or that God did not keep you from failing, sometimes miserably. God probably did not keep disease, suffering, tragedy, or death away from your door, nor did God shield you from confrontation with all the "-isms" and ill treatment of your culture. Yet as

Tamar, Rahab, Ruth, and Bathsheba discovered, so you may have discovered as well—God did keep God's promise never to leave you alone. For the female ancestors of Jesus and for you, the most important knowledge is simply this: God kept you, which was everything.

So, then, remember your mother roots.
Remember who you are.
Remember whose you are.
Remember and be thankful.

The Last Word

MARY'S "YES"

Now that we have contemplated
the intertwined mother roots of Jesus
and pondered how the possible unconscious
knowing of his ancestral mothers might have helped
prepare, shape, and define Jesus for his ministry,
we briefly turn to Mary, the mother of Jesus,
and remember her. That Mary occupies a place
separate and distinct from the other
ancestral mothers of Jesus is not breaking news.
Yet she stands beside them,
not above them.

HER BEHAVIOR, like theirs, was initially considered scandalous and immoral by some Jews and many Gentiles. Her teenage pregnancy led to charges of illegitimacy and later demands by some early religious authorities for either an explanation or punishment. But her actions became accepted, as were those of Tamar, Rahab, Ruth, and Bathsheba, as part of God's plan of salvation for humankind. History regards Mary as an obedient and willing instrument of God.

While the biblical text reveals little about Mary, more has been written about this young maiden than about any other woman throughout the history of Christianity. For at least two thousand years she has been the dominant female figure in Christian culture. Beautiful churches have been erected worldwide in her honor. Some of the world's greatest music and poetry have been inspired by her, and the Annunciation is one of the most painted scenes in the history of Western art. In our world of technology Mary even has her own Web sites where we may chat with people she has most recently visited! We are familiar with her story and may feel that we know it well. Yet we should include some of Mary's her-story in this study about the matriarchs in the life of Jesus. From the soil of her mother roots God's own holy growth sprang forth.

Take time to remember as much as you can about Mary's story in the Bible. Recall all the details you can about who she was, her description, her relationships, and when and where she lived. Then read both Annunciation stories that foretell the birth of Jesus (Matt. 1:18-25; Luke 1:26-38). In Luke's infancy narrative also read the Magnificat, or "Mary's Song" (Luke 1:46-55). What are the most striking differences you found between the two stories? How does the writer of Matthew's Gospel portray Mary? How does the writer of Luke's Gospel depict Mary? In what ways does Mary seem more active and present to the situation in one Gospel story than in the other? Why do you think the Gospel narrators interpreted Mary's role differently? In which version does Mary seem to possess the character and "chutzpah" of the other four ancestral mothers of Jesus—Matthew or Luke?

Mary in the Gospel according to Matthew

The writer of Matthew's Gospel wanted to convince the Jews who were not members of his faith community that Jesus was the promised messianic "son of David" in whom resided Emmanuel, God-with-us (Matt. 1:22-24). He begins the Gospel with a genealogy of Jesus the Messiah to make certain this point will not be missed. And he ends the Gospel with the proclamation, "Remember, I am with you always, to the end of the age" (Matt. 28:20). Everything sandwiched in between in the Gospel has to bend to this theological tenet. For the writer the "how" of Jesus' conception (virgin birth) is no more significant than the "why" of his birth (to incarnate the living presence of God-with-us). Jesus fulfilled the Hebrew Scriptures, and *how* he got here had to be balanced with *why* he came. After the infancy narrative the Gospel develops Jesus' virginal conception and birth no further. The incarnation of God-with-us in the person of Jesus is the writer's major theme.

Matthew's Gospel narrative assigns the dominant role to Joseph, not Mary. Joseph discovered that Mary, to whom he was engaged, was pregnant. Rather than first emphasize the miracle of Jesus' conception, the writer gives immediate attention to Joseph's reaction to this news. Although a righteous and just man, Joseph was bewildered and beside himself. He decided not to expose Mary to public disgrace by having her condemned to death for adultery, which his culture and the Mosaic law supported (Deut. 22:20-21). Instead, he planned quietly to send her away. In first-century Palestine these circumstances would have consigned Mary to a living death as a disobedient outcast—pregnant, unwed, oppressed, and with no future for herself or her illegitimate child.

Joseph apparently needed heavenly help to comprehend what on earth was taking place. An angel visited him in a dream and told him of Mary's conception by the Holy Spirit, instructing Joseph to name her son Jesus. The announcement of Jesus' birth was told first to Joseph, the distraught husband-to-be, rather than to the pregnant young woman, who perhaps was unaware of what had happened to her. The writer never hints that Mary knew she had conceived by the Holy Spirit, that she would give birth to a son, or that Joseph would name him Jesus. She had to wait to hear all this news from Joseph.

Many scholars believe Joseph's naming of Jesus reflects an early adoption formula commonly used during this time. A procedure of public naming would acknowledge Joseph as the legal father of Jesus. All the rights and benefits of family name and inheritance, including the link to the Davidic line, would be passed on to Jesus as if Joseph were his biological father and Jesus Joseph's legal heir. Such an adoption would provide Jesus with ancestors just as surely as biological descent. Jesus truly would be a "son of David" as well as Mary's son.

When Joseph woke from his dream, he did as the angel had commanded and took Mary as his wife. According to the scripture, the two had no sexual contact until after Jesus' birth. With the charges of illegitimacy generated by many Jews and some early Gentile Christians surrounding Jesus' birth, Mary's pregnancy had to be defended and somehow made right. Perhaps in defense against these charges the writer made a point of Joseph's strong role regarding the birth of Jesus, hoping to quell the controversy with a genealogy that included the four women we have studied along with the infancy narrative. The biblical narrative would convince dissenters that the manner of Jesus' conception fulfilled the prophecy of Hebrew Scriptures. These women and Mary were all part of God's plan for the salvation of humankind.

According to the writer, "All this took place to fulfill what had been spoken by the LORD through the prophet: 'Look, the virgin shall conceive and bear a son, and they shall name him Emmanuel,' which means, 'God is with us'" (Matt. 1:22-23). In Jesus, God was present. In using Isaiah 7:14 the writer probably meant to stress the fulfillment of God's promise to be with God's people as much as to legitimate the virginal event of Jesus' conception and birth. Any claim about Mary's conception caused by God's intervention through the Holy Spirit serves as a Christological affirmation about the identity of Jesus the Messiah rather than historical fact, an affirmation conceived by faith and born out of our personal experience.

The Matthean writer's interest in Mary seems minimal. Given a modest role, she is referred to in the angel's annunciation to Joseph and appears only briefly in the birth narrative. Neither exalted nor appearing to find much favor, Mary is not privileged to communicate with God's messenger and receives no chance to speak about or choose her course. Her feelings about Jesus' divine begetting and her attitude about Joseph's role remain unknown to us. The Gospel account evidences no empathy for her situation or admiration for her role.

If Joseph's doubt about Mary's pregnancy is a prelude to Jesus' birth, the sense of impending danger and tragedy are the postlude. Jesus' life was threatened from the beginning. No shepherds came to worship the newborn child in Matthew's Gospel. Instead Herod put a death warrant out on Jesus, so the family fled to Egypt. No heavenly choirs praised God at Jesus' birth. Instead weeping and wailing over the slaughter of innocent children engulfed Bethlehem. No celebration attended the family's return to the land of Israel. Instead the refugee family settled in rural Nazareth because Joseph feared exposure in Judea. Through all the family's travails, Joseph modeled the higher righteousness by making decisions and acting as protector of Mary and her child. Mary was portrayed as passively receptive.

Some have described Mary as a submissive vessel who simply received and let grow within her the seed planted by the Holy Spirit. While Jesus' divine begetting came without human effort, we should make no mistake about it: With human effort and by a human mother Jesus was born. In that birth and in whatever mystery of faith it held, the "how" and the "why" came together and reconciled the human and divine. The miracle of God-with-us communicated in the birth of Jesus is perpetuated day after day in the lives of those who offer themselves to God.

After Joseph moved his family to Nazareth, the Gospel writer paid little attention to Mary. With few exceptions she lingered in the background of the story. Despite her role as the mother of Emmanuel, God-with-us, Mary's importance was almost overtaken by the her-stories and personalities of the other female ancestors named in Jesus' genealogy. However, linking Mary with them as a survivor of the controversies that surrounded her situation—including Joseph's first impulse to send her away—provides testimony to God's loving-kindness. God sided with these women, whose her-stories have a fundamental place in God's salvation history of humankind.

Mary in the Gospel according to Luke

To encounter a Mary more like the ancestral mothers depicted in Jesus' genealogy, we turn to the Gospel according to Luke. Here Mary comes alive and chooses for herself how she will make the most of an unconventional situation. In this Gospel the writer tells a different story about Mary, the central character and a hearer and doer of God's word.

In Luke's Gospel the angel Gabriel announces the coming

birth of a son to Mary and tells her the name by which the child is to be known. Rather than being found sleeping or dreaming, Mary is wide awake in this account. She has an extended conversation with the angel about her conception and the role of the Holy Spirit and about the nature and mission of her son. Even before Jesus' conception God's purpose was revealed to Mary, and through the Holy Spirit she knew that the power of God would make it happen. Mary believed before the fact. This conception was no accident, this birth no mistake. Both were divinely ordained. This Gospel contains no sense of impending doom. Instead good news too wonderful to be kept a secret prompts Mary to sing a song of praise as she celebrates her pregnancy with her relative Elizabeth.

Luke's Gospel gives us little information about Joseph in the birth and infancy narratives. We are told that he was from the house of David and that Mary was engaged to him. He went to Bethlehem with Mary to register for the first census. Although they were engaged, she was expecting a child not his own. Not Mary but Joseph is the passive presence throughout. His is a shadow personality who never emerges into the full light of God's wondrous activity. The writer of Matthew's Gospel depicts Joseph as a doubting husband-to-be (albeit a good and righteous man) about to put Mary out on the streets until God intervenes. But Luke's Gospel account includes a supportive Joseph because Mary needs a husband to adopt Jesus as his legal heir, and Jesus needs a genealogy that connects him to the house of David (Luke 1:32-33, 69).

Not until after Jesus begins his ministry at age thirty does the writer of Luke's Gospel record his genealogy (Luke 3:23-38). Jesus "was the son [as was thought] of Joseph," descended from a royal lineage through David, an Israelite lineage through Abraham, and a universal human lineage through Adam, the first earthling, and finally from God. Instead of attempting to prove the Jewish lineage of Jesus as the fulfillment of Hebrew Scriptures as did Matthew's genealogy, in Luke's genealogy Jesus is born into and emerges as the son of God from our common humanity. What God had promised to Abraham and David was about to be fulfilled in ways that neither of them would have imagined. Jesus' fulfillment of his identity as God's Beloved would surprise and shock the Jews, the Gentiles, and the people who would later call themselves Christians.

Noticeably absent from Luke's genealogy are the names of any women, including Mary, as if there were no mother roots connecting Jesus to his female ancestors. Yet in the Annunciation and infancy stories we come to know Mary as the mother of the Savior of the world who rooted him solidly in nourishing soil. Within the Lukan Gospel, Mary is the only woman who asks questions (Luke 1:34; 2:48) and the only woman who is given a full speech of proclamation (Luke 1:46-55).

Throughout the ages Christian interpretation of Mary in the New Testament has held that she represented all the best qualities found in Jewish womanhood and motherhood. Deeply and spiritually sensitive, she served as a model disciple, exhibiting purity, faith, and obedience to God's will. She attended to her son's religious training as she honored the Jewish tradition; and even when she lacked understanding, she remained loyal to her son's mission. In a stable she wrapped him in swaddling clothes at his birth, and at his death on the cross she watched as he was wrapped in burial cloths and laid in a borrowed tomb.

According to the writer of Luke's Gospel, the Holy Spirit and prayer were active ingredients throughout the Gospel story and in the lives of both Mary and Jesus. The Holy Spirit had been at work in Mary from the beginning of the Annunciation and infancy narratives. In response to Elizabeth's inspired words and while Jesus rested in her womb, Mary prayed to God a song of praise that would usher in a new age. Throughout his life and ministry Jesus was grounded in the empowering presence of the Holy Spirit through prayer. After his baptism the Holy Spirit descended upon him, and a voice from heaven said, "You are my Son, the Beloved; with you I am well pleased" (Luke 3:21-22). The Holy Spirit anointed Jesus in Nazareth for his ministry (Luke 4:18). We are told Jesus prayed often and without ceasing and taught those who followed him how to pray. His last instruction to his disciples was to wait until they had been gifted with the Holy Spirit and "clothed with power from on high" before they attempted to continue their work (Luke 24:49).

The faithful followers of Jesus waited in Jerusalem, among them Mary and certain other women. While praying in an upper room, the men and the women were overshadowed by the Holy Spirit, which came upon them and empowered them to conceive and give birth to a new thing, the church (Acts 2:1-4). Mary had been overshadowed by the Holy Spirit with the conception of Jesus when her-story begins. It ends with the conception of the church. What was conceived and born both times in Mary's presence was holy and wholly God's.

Mary's "Yes"

Read Luke 1:26-55 again. Imagine that you are Mary in the presence of Gabriel the great archangel. What is your response on hearing Gabriel's message for the first time? How do you feel and what do you think about the angel's invitation to you? As we move further into Mary's her-story, remember the other female ancestors of Jesus. Even as her scandalous pregnancy disturbed the air around Mary, the air had already been disturbed centuries before by the other ancestral mothers. And with each disturbance came fresh air and new life. With the coming of Jesus into the world, the familiar disturbances turned into a mighty rushing wind. The Holy Spirit set loose continues to blow where it will.

The branches of Jesus' family tree, grown tall from the ancestral mother roots, still bend softly in the gentle breeze of hospitality and loving-kindness and whip furiously about in the storms of prejudice and hatred. God's involvement in human affairs always disturbs the air around us. We have no reason to suppose that God will stop disturbing us now or in the future. God comes searching for us, ready or not, while we wait to be found. The strange twist is that God, the one on whom we thought we were waiting, is already waiting for us. God waits for us to say yes. Even though we may not fully understand where this response will take us and even though some of us will resist, still God waits for our yes.

Centuries ago a young maiden engaged to be married went about her ordinary routines, waiting for life to catch up with her dreams—the stuff of gossamer threads spun into the fabric of marriage, children, and security. She arose one day as always, expecting that her world and all that was commonplace in it would remain the same. But this day would differ from any day before or after. The air around her was disturbed by an annunciation, an announcement; and God waited for Mary to say yes.

Do you recall Mary's first response after the angel Gabriel's greeting? She was silent. Much perplexed and deeply distressed by the angel's words, she pondered what sort of greeting this might be. The air around Mary had been disturbed, and she respected the mystery with silence. She took time to reflect, to consider, to wonder, to think things through before answering. Mary was not about to be rushed into giving a hurried answer—even by an angel!

We can imagine Gabriel shifting from one foot to the other, wing feathers ruffled, uneasy with Mary's pondering. In the silence the angel may have thought this was not quite the response he had anticipated. Perhaps no longer able to keep still and hoping to convince Mary to give her answer, Gabriel said, "Do not be afraid, Mary, for you have found favor with God."

"Do not be afraid," said the larger-than-life archangel to a young girl not much older than a child. Who holds the balance of power in this conversation? "Do not be afraid, Mary, even though you are about to conceive and bear an illegitimate child who will be called the Son of God. Do not be afraid, even though the child will rule over a kingdom without end. Do not be afraid, even though the Holy Spirit will overshadow you, whatever that means. Do not be afraid." Easy enough for an angel to say, but it may not have sounded all that comforting to Mary. Favor with God, especially when announced by an angel, was enough to instill fear in anyone!

Mary might have remembered the stories of her religious heritage and wondered what it really meant to find favor with God. She might have known the story of Abel's being killed by Cain because Abel was favored of God. Maybe she imagined what Sarah, pregnant at ninety because God favored her, must have experienced. She might have recalled Abraham, favored by God yet commanded to sacrifice his only son, whose birth he had awaited for decades. Perhaps she remembered Joseph, the favorite one, sold into slavery by his brothers. Moses found favor with God and died trying to get into the Promised Land. Tamar, Rahab, Ruth, and Bathsheba found favor with God, but they suffered betrayal, deaths, scandals, and isolation. Naomi found favor with God, and her pleasantness turned to bitterness. Faithful Job, favored by God, lost everything he possessed. The Israelites, God's own people, wandered in the wilderness for forty years. And now Mary was being told that she had found favor with God. Small wonder that this possibility did not sound particularly appealing to her. Perhaps what troubled Mary most was the thought of what might happen to her if she did say yes. Finding favor? What might it mean?

The angel continued to speak with Mary about what would come to pass. She listened as Gabriel told her she would know the truth of his message when she conceived and bore a son whom she would name Jesus. He told her about the greatness of her son, and she listened. Mary knew the correct order of events: marriage, pregnancy, and then birth. What Gabriel proposed reversed all her expectations and dreams.

Before Mary answered Gabriel, she asked him a question, a rather gutsy thing to do. To ask a question not just of an angel, but of a mighty archangel! Her direct and pointed question was a practical one, an inquiry about something she perceived to be humanly impossible: "How can this be, since I am a virgin?" She said in effect, "I am not even married. I have no husband." She demanded a straight answer from an angel, and up to this point in Mary's herstory, she had yet to agree to anything. The angel did not really answer her question, explaining neither "how" such a miracle could be or "how" it would happen—only that it would be. Through the power of the Holy Spirit, the signature of God would be upon the child Mary was to conceive, and the child would be holy and called the Son of God.

Was Mary's silence due to her fear? Could she still have been calculating the consequences of her yes? Was finding favor with God worth being disfavored and discredited by others? How would Joseph, the man to whom she was engaged, respond? Would he believe her? What would she tell her mother? her friends? the synagogue officials? How long could she keep her pregnancy secret? What would she feel in her body when this change came about? Who would ever believe such a strange story? If your daughter or sister or granddaughter came home pregnant with an explanation like this, would you believe it?

To be a betrothed virgin meant that the woman was already considered the man's possession. Her life belonged to him. If an engaged woman was raped or suspected of infidelity, or worse yet, if she became pregnant, she was considered damaged goods—of little value. Her husband-to-be could have her punished, or if he chose, have her put to death by stoning. At the very least, the culture would expect him to send her away. If Mary were to make the outrageous claim that she was pregnant with God's own son, the religious leaders would have charged her with blasphemy against God and would undoubtedly have imposed a death sentence.

Mary asked only one question of the angel, but surely she must have had more. Perhaps she wondered if she could really trust God with her very life. Could she trust God enough to say yes? Was her faith flexible enough to believe without guarantees? In the future would her favor with the Almighty be remembered? If she said no, how would her future change? Would the angel look for some other young maiden who would say yes to God's strange invitation? Was she the first to be asked, or had Gabriel approached others before her? Did she really have a choice in the matter?

God took a great risk in our creation by giving us the freedom of choice. God's invitation through the angel left room for Mary to choose. Just as we have the freedom to say no to God, so did Mary have room to decline the invitation. God does not coerce, and Mary could still refuse.

Without freedom of choice, Mary's response makes little sense. Mary as victim of a coercive, demanding, threatening God is not the same Mary who freely chooses to join with God to liberate the wretched of the earth. Once Mary said yes, God acted through her body to create a place for God's own holy birthing. The spirit took hold in her flesh and thickened into life. Impregnated by God's Word spoken to her, Mary spoke her own revolutionary word about turning the world around and upside down. Her risk-taking yes empowered her to proclaim with tough authority the truth that the world and the church still find hard to hear. God has scattered the arrogant, overthrown those in power, and given the marginalized freedom from systemic injustice. God has given the hungry good things, but the rich God has sent away empty.

Mary saw a clear connection between the spiritual realm of God and the social, economic, religious, and political realities of the world. Her proclamation aimed at restructuring the institutions and orders that rejected the poor and excluded the hungry. Mary may have known about keeping a clean house, but what she spoke of amounted to more than just shaking the rugs and dusting the furniture. She spoke of a thorough housecleaning for the house of Israel that would shake the familiar and comfortable foundations. Mary spoke this message even before God's son was born. Mary introduced the key themes of Jesus' preaching while Jesus was still in her womb. Before he had the power of speech, Mary had already given voice to his life's mission.

Mary disturbed the air with her hymn of praise. She hit every note of life, singing in every key about a new creation, a new way of risk taking and becoming, a new way of committing ourselves to one another and to the world. Mary's yes sings of liberation and transformation, of reform and reversal, of change upon change until a new order of peace and justice for all is established.

Jesus' radical life began at home with the model of radicality established by his mother, who had the courage to say yes to God. But she does not stand alone. A yes to God's invitation had already been spoken down through the ages and across the span of generations by the female ancestors of Jesus. Their yes announced beginnings and endings, birth and death, waiting and fulfillment, the end of an old age and the beginning of a new. The yes of Mary and Tamar, Rahab, Ruth, and Bathsheba continues on through us as we struggle with what it means to find favor with God. The world stands on tiptoe waiting for us to become more fully the radical yes-sayers God has invited us to become.

When Mary said yes, she could not have known about the silent night of birth in a stable or the angelic hosts singing and praising God. Would she have known about the visit to the Temple with twelve-year-old Jesus? Could she have foreseen that her son would willingly place himself in harm's way for the sake of others? Would she have said yes if she had known about the betrayal of her son that would lead to his public scourging or his trip to Calvary and crucifixion? Mary only knew for certain that if she said yes to God, everything would change. And so it will be with our yes.

An old age may end and a new age begin with the yes we speak. In the places where we give birth to our holy imaginations, God may take root in our hearts. Impregnated by God's holy Word, the wombs of radical hope may yet blossom and bless our efforts to build a world of justice and peace. Each time we say yes, the Holy Spirit overshadows us and something new comes to birth in us.

Our Christian roots are intertwined with the female ancestors of Jesus and planted deep in the soil of his family tree. Tamar, Rahab, Ruth, Bathsheba, and Mary courageously disturbed the air around them. Heirs to their faithfulness, we are called to do the same when we answer yes. Perhaps not yet fully comprehending what our yes may mean, but in faith that surpasses our knowledge and trusting God with our very lives, may we boldly say with Mary:

> "Here am I, the servant of the LORD;
> let it be with me according to your word."
> So be it. Amen.

ANOTHER BOOK BY
HELEN BRUCH PEARSON

DO WHAT YOU HAVE THE POWER TO DO
Studies of Six New Testament Women

BASED ON six biblical stories of encounters between Jesus and unnamed women, this study invites and challenges us to move closer toward the community Jesus envisioned. Each session guides us through five steps of study:

- exploration
- meditation
- encounter
- interrogative
- closing worship